Hasta La Vista
California

Tear down that "immoral wall," and give California its independence.

Why do so many people seem to hate California? This book tells you why!

I am beginning to see two competing hate groups in America. The first of course consists of the MSNBC and CNN leftist crowds that hate Trump more than anything in their lives. The other is the hate I learned about in researching this book. In a nutshell it is the hate that Republicans in California and the people like me in *flyover country,* who have learned enough about life in California to have developed a deep dislike, if not a real hate for the Golden State.

Over a year ago on my birthday, Author Mike McPhate asked: "Is it the traffic? The air pollution? The crazy housing costs?" Yes! Yes! Yes! And more. Paul Chabot, the founder of Conservative Move, a company that helps disgruntled Californians start new lives in the country's red states added his two cents: "Politics is what has really ruined the state." When pollsters in 2012 asked American voters about whether they liked each state, California came in dead last. It is not a joke. It is real!

Americans hate California. It is clear. Republicans, suffering a 46-7 minority in the US House are far more likely than Democrats to hate the Golden State. Take your own survey and you too will find out that a lot of people in California hate California. Of course, I am talking about the governmental entity controlled by the buffoons in Sacramento, not the people—though they are Democrats. What better reason to simply give them an Arnold Schwarzenegger sendoff with an introduction by Rocky Stallone. Here it is:

Yo, Hasta La Vista Baby! For America, this means "Hasta La Vista California, and the sooner the better."

For me and many Americans there will be no remorse and Californians themselves are ready to kick America out of California with its Calexit secession movement.

Instead of *Hasta La Vista,* I would give odds that a poll of the other 49 states would suggest a different sendoff message and that these Americans would never look back on the quickest good-by in history. "Yo, Good Riddance California." Get yourselves a passport to visit the United States of America.

Besides living with insane Democrat policies, American workers have a natural disdain for the state because they are against illegal immigration because it redistributes wealth from those who compete with immigrants to those who use immigrants—from the employee to the employer. There are lots of other reasons to say Hasta La Vista and this books hits on most of them. Grab a copy of this book from Amazon online or another bookseller, get yourself a few cold ones on ice, and settle in your easy chair for a read that will take less than a day, and learn what to do if you live in California and what to watch out for if you live in the "Other 49." You'll love this book.

**LETS
GO
PUBLISH**

BRIAN W. KELLY

Referenced Material: *The information in this book has been obtained through personal and third-party observations, interviews, and copious research. Where unique information has been provided or extracted from other sources, those sources are acknowledged within the text of the book itself or at the end of the chapter in the Sources Section. Thus, there are no formal footnotes nor is there a bibliography section. Any picture that does not have a source was taken from various sites on the Internet with no credit attached. If resource owners would like credit in the next printing, please email publisher.*

Published by: LETS GO PUBLISH!
Publisher & Editor: Brian P. Kelly
Email: info@letsgopublish.com
                        www.letsgopublish.com
Book Cover Design   Brian W. Kelly;
Editing   Brian P. Kelly
Library of Congress Copyright Information Pending

ISBN Information: The International Standard Book Number (ISBN) is a unique machine-readable identification number, which marks any book unmistakably. The ISBN is the clear standard in the book industry. 159 countries and territories are officially ISBN members.

The Official ISBN For this book is **978-1-947402-82-9**

The price for this work is : $12.95 USD

10   9   8   7   6   5   4   3   2   1

Release Date: April 2019

LETS
GO
PUBLISH

Dedication

I dedicate this book

To my wonderful children—Brian, Mike, and Katie, and their wonderful mother, Patricia.

We are a close family and our children help in every way they can to assure the muse is always fired up.

Thank you all!

Acknowledgments

In every book that I write or edit, I publicly acknowledged all the help that I have received from many sources. Some of these wonderful people are still living on earth and others have made their way to heaven.

I would like to thank many people for helping me in this effort.

I have listed their names on www.letsgopublosh.com. The story I tell on the Lets Go Publish! Web site is about all the helpers I have. On the site, look for the main menu on the left side. Please take a run out there and you will find the text about all of those who are acknowledged for their help in bringing my books to you.

God bless you all for your help.

My plan is to make necessary changes to the acknowledgments on the LGP web site as often as I can so that I can update the status of the many who for so long helped me with my books.

Thank you all for all your help in keeping Lets Go Publish and the folks at Amazon, (www.amazon.com/author/brianwkelly) on the top of the heap for so long.

Thank you all on the big list in the sky.

In this book, I received some extra special help from many friends including Dennis Grimes, Gerry Rodski, Joyce (the Scrapper) Heck, Wily Ky Eyely, Angel Irene McKeown Kelly, Angel Edward Joseph Kelly Sr., Angel Edward Joseph Kelly Jr., Ann Flannery, Angel James Flannery Sr., Mary Daniels, Bill Daniels, Robert Garry Daniels, Angel Sarah Janice Daniels, Joe Kelly and Diane Kelly, Angel Joe McKeown Jr., Angel, Teddy Sydleski, and angel Jim Faller. These other angels were very instrumental. Angel Punkie Daniels, Angels Phoebe, Breezie, Brady and Ben Kelly, .

To sum up my acknowledgments, as I do in every book that I have written, I am compelled to offer that I am truly convinced that "the only thing one can do alone in life is fail." Thanks to my family, good friends, and a wonderful helping team, I am not alone.

Thank you all

Brian W. Kelly

Table of Contents

Preface:

As a Democrat, like many other one-time Democrats, I saw the Party leave me. I did not have to leave the Democrat Party. Democrats do not know how to legislate whether they control Sacramento, New York, or Detroit. Democrats worked hard to blacken the name Republican while destroying whatever it is they choose to touch.

Perhaps if the Republicans changed the name of their party to The American Party or to the John Doe Party and they got rid of the elite swamp rats, and became a force for good instead of behaving like wimps, Democrat regulars would begin to join in droves and make the new party unbeatable and unafraid. Right now, there is no good home for misplaced, unrepresented Democrats. But, there could be.

To this day, the cold and clammy and corrupt press or as Trump calls them, *the fake news media*, have recoiled, rendering only soft vollies because they now fear that AG Barr may begin to put them and their ilk in jail for a long-time. Those of us who like how the country is moving with Trump at the helm, are recharged knowing that finally having a tough American as an AG that is non-partisan will help America in a big way. Soon, AG Barr will get to the bottom of why a fake illegal investigation was ever commissioned. Hopefully it is over. Would it not be nice if California found a guy like Trump or Reagan again or a straight shooter like William Barr to steer that big ship?

California once had it all. God created the Golden State as a land flowing with milk and honey? What happened? Did mankind destroy it or just the Democrat part of mankind.

As I write this book on permitting California to permanently sign off from the United States, the winter season is over and Spring has just begun. Spring is the season that brings back the sights and fragrances that help us recall the biblical image of a perfect land that could have once been California.

The captivating green hills flow with honey dripping from its hives, like liquid gold in the sunlight. A spacious land full of the colors of the flag is covered with red cyclamen, white rockrose, and flowering Blue Jacaranda blooms. There are also the flowers of California's myriad wild fruits, and the warm valley air smelling of their nectar. Amen!

Where else in the nation can a single property owner such as one in San Diego on a simple 60 X 100 lot with a nice American Craftsman home with a small driveway, have a lime tree, a lemon tree, and an orange tree as well as an attractive chicken coop with chickens providing great eggs on a daily basis. Folks, you'd be talking about California--one of a kind. From the tall trees to the golden seacoast to the fertile farmland—one of a kind. Simple and fancy—one of a kind. How could man destroy such wonder?

Is it possible for man to take what God has made and destroy it by trying to save it or is the plot in California unintentional? I am just finishing the reading of a little post that shows a lot of worry about whether a once most beautiful state—California—can be sustained. The fear is that goofy men and women called Democrats continue legislating with an insane hand. The title of the piece I read is called *"How California Democrats Have Turned The Golden State Into A 'Sh*thole."*

The following text was posted by Katy Grimes at 1:03 am on Jan 17, 2018. The situation is so bleak for those of us who once loved to visit California, many of us have decided never to go back. Only California could take milk and honey, and without ever combining the two, and from that produce a land flowing of feces and urine.

By the way Katy Grimes, the Editor of the California Globe, is a long-time Investigative Journalist covering the California State Capitol. She is the co-author of California's War Against Donald Trump: Who Wins? Who Loses?

Here is the blurb from her Trump book:

"California's War Against Donald Trump" takes a thorough, analytical look into the clash between Donald Trump's policies and those of California's liberal leaders who have mounted a vigorous "resistance," and reveals just who is winning, and losing, from all the political grandstanding. With hundreds of references cited, dealing with subjects spanning sanctuary city policies, to "The Wall," to healthcare, education, the temporary travel ban, federal regulatory policy, thwarting enforcement of immigration laws, and especially climate change, the battle between liberal Democrats in Sacramento and Trump and the

Republicans in control in Washington, D.C. is vividly detailed, from a perspective that agrees with Trump that California is "out of control," and that politicians would do much better for the state by dropping the hostility and finding some sort of common ground."

But, nobody anywhere expects that ever to happen.

Grimes asks: "How many ways can California's leftist Democrats turn the Golden State into a sh*thole?" I will be focusing on some of her writing from Part II of her post in this preface. In Part 1 of her post, she addressed the outbound migration of California's hard-working middle class, as well as millennials now choosing low-tax states to live and work. Despite this, California's ruling party is doubling down on business-destroying policies, energy destroying policies, education destroying policies, and policies destroying California's abundant natural resources. God's gifts are being put asunder.

Governor Moonbeam, similar to the Tin Man in the Wizard of Oz is asking God for a brain instead of a heart. God seemingly took the request in the most positive light according to Gavin Newsom and he gave Newsom to leftist California to have and to hold until the Death of California forces a parting. Newsom so far is operating as a Moonbeam clone.

Katy Grimes

Grimes offers her proof beginning below with examples to make one wonder why each legislator in California does not have a person with a white coat following their every move. Maybe they do? It is no wonder the state is short on doctors.

California recently just passed a law prohibiting routine use of antibiotics on livestock in the state. Former Governor Jerry Brown wanted to ban the sale of gas- and diesel-powered cars in California. Brown is gone but not forgotten. The state Public Utilities Commission's decided to close Diablo Canyon nuclear power plant, marking the end of more than a half-century of clean nuclear power generation in the state. California lawmakers passed a vehicle registration fee increase, as high as $175 for many cars. Will illegal aliens find government subsidies to afford the fee?

California is now a Sanctuary State, harboring millions of illegal aliens, and preventing immigration officers from easily accessing criminal illegal aliens in jails and prisons.

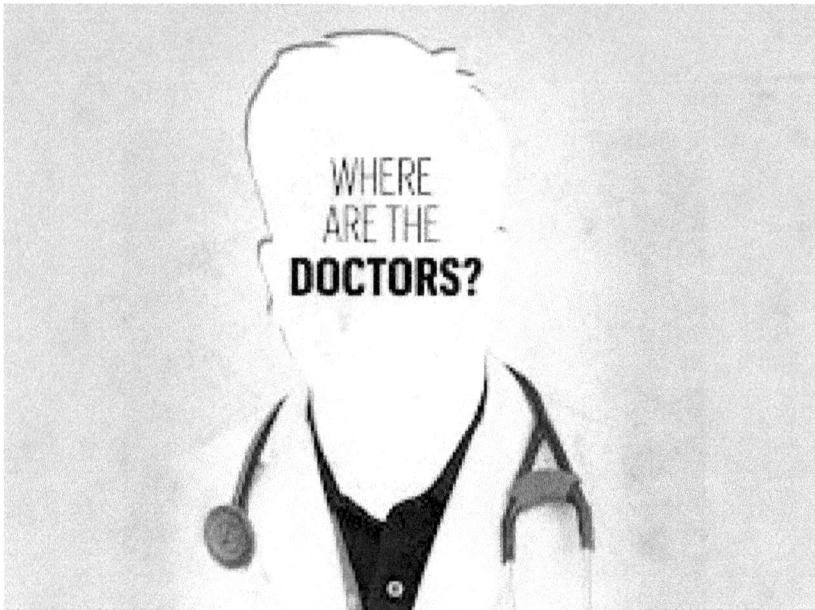

WHERE ARE THE **DOCTORS?**

The state no longer has a high school exit exam in California, because so many students could not pass the easy test during the four years in high school. So leftist Democrats decided to do away with the test, rather than address the state's failing schools. Grimes' son passed the exit exam in 9th grade.

California's pet stores are now banned from selling dogs, cats and rabbits unless they are rescue animals. So much for free market principles. Can it be because they eat as the state does not seem to have a problem with animal waster products including humans.

Employers will no longer be able to ask job applicants about their salary history, compensation or benefits.

California community colleges are now free for first-time college students. Hmmm. Who is paying for this?

Because of "declining voter turnout," neighborhood polling places will be replaced with elections by mail in California. No fraud here…

The State of California Agricultural Labor Relations Board is in collusion with the United Farm Workers labor union to force the state's largest non-union farming companies into union contracts. Jerry

Brown's corrupt California Supreme Court recently ruled that forced collective bargaining is constitutional. Absolutely mind boggling.

California's explosion of homeless people is largely thanks to Governor Jerry Brown's prison "realignment" scheme, and two propositions which redefined many serious crimes to justify letting hardened criminals and habitual repeat offenders out of jails and prisons. The realignment scheme was so bad, the Legislature then had to pass another bill redefining "recidivism."

-- End of Grimes' post --

As ridiculousness, insanity, and asininity mark the most significant achievements of lawmakers in the Golden State, the press is cheering how the powerful Democrats have silenced the voices of values-oriented Republicans:

As veteran California political writer Dan Walters of The Sacramento Bee put it: "The election saw the emergence of a much different demographic profile that, if it continues, permanently changes assumptions about our politics. California's new electorate, derived from exit polling data, is multiracial, younger, more liberal, not very religious and less likely to be married with children. ... The long reign of older white voters is coming to an end. ... " 'Thank God.'

Yes indeed, folks, like Logan's Run where at 30 you became eligible to become soylent green; or a new version of *Kill white guys for being guilty of "breathing while white,"* the "long reign of older white voters is coming to an end." I wonder how that makes the old white farts feel in California. Time to go to Texas?

By the way, the term *Soylent Green* some may recall is taken from a 70's film. Soylent Green is a supposedly soy and lentil-based nutrition source which later turns out to be made out of harvested humans hence the quote "Soylent green is people" Is that where we are heading—to a land where all the milk and honey are gone and corpses provide the only nutrition? Those old white guys may soon be sold in Super Markets?

Americans hate California more than ever. Take a survey and you will find out that a lot of people in California also hate California. In a recent USA survey, for example, about who likes which states, California came in dead last. Maybe its time has come.

I am talking about the governmental entity controlled by the buffoons in Sacramento, not all the regular people—though there are far too many Democrats for anybody's good. What better reason to simply give them an Arnold Schwarzenegger sendoff with an introduction by Rocky Stallone.

Yo, Hasta La Vista Baby! That means "*Hasta La Vista California*, and the sooner the better."

After the quick good-byes, for me and many Americans there will be no remorse and Californians themselves are ready to kick America out of California with their Calexit secession movement.

Many people inside California and outside of the state are sick of its anti-people policies. Smarter Californians continue to leave the state because it's over-taxed, over-regulated and over-managed by the worst political class in America. The voters will have no one to blame but themselves when it all falls apart.

Will the rest of the states gladly pick up the massive debt that the Golden State hopes to dump on the rest of us?. I don't think so. It is highly unlikely the states will not engage the baboons in Congress if they decide to bail out California. After all, its government has made El Dorado *unsustainable*. Giving California a loan would be like dumping cash off a cliff—good money after bad.

Those of us in the "Other 49" are not interested in being stiffed by the Gold Coast and we want none of the negatives that might come our way from Big Cal disappearing overnight. We'd love to look west and see no USA California. Calexit would ensure that taxpayers in the remaining 49 states would not be forced to bail out decades of California profligacy.

Some Cal cities are more infamous in their disregard for sanitary living than others. For example, one of the most beautiful cities in the country (at one time), has turned into a dumping ground for Bay Area bowel movements -- and things have gotten so bad the California city is now dubbed the "Doo-Doo Capital in the U.S." Californians are not laughing about it. But rather than solve the problem, instead their small minds have chosen to out signs warning people of the feces, urine and needles in certain sections. Solving problems is not a Democrat strong point.

Your author, Brian W. Kelly for years has monitored what is happening to regular Americans and has written extensively on this major problem with the Republican Party as well as the now completely unhinged, incompetent Democrats.

He and those of us now reading this book know that Democrats keep surprising even those of us who have lost all faith in them. Democrats in Sacramento and wherever they have control, are not about to ever stop their insane ways. We have seen the new radical anti-capitalist, infanticide advocating, Anti-American cowardly Democrats, and they are ugly for sure. Today, there are more of them in California than anywhere else in the nation.

Kelly is one of America's most outspoken and eloquent conservative speakers and authors on American values. He is the author of 198 books including *Saving America The Trump Way*; *Why Trump?*; *Taxation without Representation*; *Obama's Seven Deadly Sins*; *Kill the EPA! Jobs! Jobs! Jobs!* and many other fine patriotic books.

All Kelly books are now available at Amazon, and Kindle. Many can be found at Barnes & Noble and other fine booksellers. Enjoy your next read, please! www.amazon.com/author/brianwkelly.

Thanks to you, Hasta La Vista California is about to appear at the top of America's most read list.

Sincerely,

Brian P. Kelly, Editor

About the Author

Brian W. Kelly retired as an Assistant Professor in the Business Information Technology (BIT) program at Marywood University, where he also served as the IBM i and midrange systems technical advisor to the IT faculty. Kelly designed, developed, and taught many college and professional courses. He is also a contributing technical editor to a number of IT industry magazines, including "The Four Hundred" and "Four Hundred Guru" published by IT Jungle.

Kelly is a former IBM Senior Systems Engineer and he has been a candidate for US Congress and the US Senate from Pennsylvania. He has an active information technology consultancy. He is the author of 198 books and numerous articles about current IT issues and general topics. For years, Brian was a frequent speaker at COMMON, IBM conferences, and other technical conferences, & user group meetings across the US. Ask him to talk at your next Tea Party or John Doe Club meeting!

Over the past ten years, Brian Kelly has become one of America's most outspoken and eloquent conservative protagonists. Besides this book, Kelly has also written _Taxation Without Representation_, _Obama's Seven Deadly Sins_, _Healthcare Accountability_, _Kill the EPA_, _Jobs! Jobs! Jobs!_, _Saving America_, _RRR_, _Why Trump?_, and many other books designed to help America and Americans.

Endorsed by the Independence Hall Tea Party in 2010, Kelly ran for Congress against a 13-term Democrat and, took no campaign contributions, spent enough to buy signs and T-shirts, and as a virtual unknown, he captured 17% of the vote—www.briankellyforcongress.com.

Chapter 1. Do Americans Hate California?

Neverland is just one part of Lalaland, which itself is a euphemism for California. Whereas Neverland has been abandoned and thus vacant for ten years, since 2009, La La Land is still functioning, controlled by a group of imbeciles in Sacramento.

We're going to do a little defining here before we get on with the big story of the hate. Lalaland as everybody knows is a colloquial term for "being out of touch with reality," usually due to bliss or ignorance. As La La Land, it is a nickname for Los Angeles, California. For our purposes in this book either version, Lalaland or La La Land is used to refer to California USA.

LA of course is Los Angeles but with the Cretins in Sacramento running the state government of California, we take the liberty of extending both terms to the full state and not just Los Angeles. Hollywood, which is more like Lalaland than anything else, is where thousands of rich and famous and fake actors play fake people in fake stories in fake settings throughout the state. It is just 6.5 miles / 19 minutes from LA.

There are no laws keeping the fake characters from polluting the rest of the state with their ignorance. They have done so and have changed the Golden State forever. Thus, the terms *La La Land* and *Lalaland* equally apply to each other and they also apply equally to the rest of the biggest state in the union.

Americans of all nationalities, cultures, races, and religions have recently been expressing their hate California for similar reasons. Take a survey and you will find out that a lot of people in California itself hate California. Of course, I am talking about the governmental entity controlled by the buffoons in Sacramento, not the people—though we know most are Democrats. What better reason to simply give them an Arnold Schwarzenegger sendoff with an introduction by Rocky Stallone. Here it is:

Yo, Hasta La Vista Baby! For America, this means "Hasta La Vista California, and the sooner the better."

For me and many other Americans there will be no remorse when the secession takes place and Californians themselves kick America out of California. All they should need is a fully executed Calexit secession agreement. The eradication of California as a state by secession is not to be confused with the plot in the original 1978 Superman movie. Some may remember that Lex Luther planned to split apart the country at the San Andreas fault-line by blowing it up.

Of course, the resulting explosion would have provided Nevada with a fine west coastline and it would have sent the entire California coastline and its inhabitants to murky ocean depths. We're not talking about anything so drastic and dastardly with Calexit but the political results will be the same.

Instead of *Hasta La Vista*, I would give odds that a poll of the other 49 states would suggest a different sendoff message. Americans from flyover country would never look back on the quickest good-by in history. "Yo, Good Riddance California." Get yourselves a passport to visit the United States of America if you find something here you crave.

If in the future, the US ever happens to desire to create another state, after granting separation permission to the 31st state, the new state if ever it comes to be, can carry the same 31st state designation. In this way, the hole in the numbering would be the last vestige of California as we know it today. It would be gone and replaced and thus gone forever. Hey why not even let the new state take on the old state's many nicknames including the Golden State, even if it may be north of Saskatchewan or South of Venezuela.

After the midterms in 2018, Republicans in Big Cal were diminished to almost nothing. At the end of the day, they controlled just seven of California's fifty-three US Congressional seats. Republicans are well aware of this perilous state of affairs. Even before it got this bad, in 2012, Sen. Lindsey Graham (R-S.C.) said: "The demographics race we're losing badly. We're not generating enough angry white guys to stay in business for the long term." In California, the handwriting suggests soon it will be 53 to zero.

California, more than any other state, has been waging an ongoing battle against Trump over illegal immigration, sanctuary state status, and the border wall. Outsiders now look at the state as more Mexifornia than California. Mexifornia is a mostly derogatory term for California's having become increasingly Mexican in population and culture, especially due to illegal immigration.

American workers are against illegal immigration among other things because it redistributes wealth from those who compete with immigrants to those who use immigrants—from the employee to the employer. For me, the claims that it is racial bias causing the actions of America—they are all wet.

California shows as much disdain for America as America for California. For example, new Governor Gavin Newsom announced on Feb. 15, 2019 that his state was about to sue America and President Donald Trump over the national emergency declaration.

As opposed to a sign of a good neighbor relationship, this is the 46th legal challenge to Trump administration policies from the Golden State. Looks like Big Cal is looking for an easy Calexit.

This time, Newsom said, the state intends to contest Trump's use of executive power for what the governor calls a manufactured crisis at the border. "Our message back to the White House is simple and clear: California will see you in court," Newsom said.

People in California are sick of its anti-people policies and they now have only one option—get out of Dodge. So, they continue to leave the state in increasing numbers because it is over-taxed, over-regulated and over-managed by the worst political class in America. The voters will have no one to blame but themselves when the cheap glue that holds it together falls apart.

California has known about its indigenous problems for years, and it has collected a ton of taxes to pay for them. The problems never get fixed. Instead, the incompetent, Democrat legislature continually diverts more than $2 billion a year to other things. That's called fraud. They know it. We know it. They keep doing it. California keeps electing them for more terms. Democrats do not change methods unless they must. Voting them back into office has ruined the state as it was and continues to be the wrong message for corrupt politicians.

Since 2004, California has lost over a million people. That is no small potatoes. The loss continues. The decrease so far represents a $26 billion net income loss. And, since 2008, based on data from relocation experts, more than 10,000 businesses have chosen to either flee from the state's restrictions or reduce their investments. They include such household names as Northrop-Grumman, Carl's Jr, Toyota and other names you would quickly recognize. The powers that be remain undaunted at their losses. With Newsom in control, taxes are going up and up and up. Soda, water, guns, and tires: They are all about to get special taxes if California Democrats have their way.

Right now, the Golden State is enjoying a tech boom. But it is not expected to last. What's good is good just for now. Recent trends in Silicon Valley—the San Diego's real estate market indicate its profitability for tech-focused investors. The median sales price in the City's office sector, for example, increased by nearly 230 percent between 2014 and 2017, and median sale prices of multifamily properties have grown every year since the recession. This is not typical for the rest of the state.

Though San Diego and the Silicon Valley may not be on par with San Francisco's expansion, the area's STEM-oriented infrastructure and massive millennial population growth rate show considerable potential moving forward. And it's a safe bet for investors, as the city saw a 95.4% occupancy rate in 2015 and has been growing since then. As wealthy taxpayers and businesses continue to flee the state, however, many ask, who will pay all its bills? Tech cannot sustain the whole state. Jerry Brown never figured it out and Gavin Newsom seems to have no clue.

Will the rest of the US states gladly pick up the massive debt so the Golden State will agree to stay connected to mainline USA? It is highly unlikely the states will not engage Congress regarding any bail-out for California. After all, its government has made El Dorado *unsustainable so giving California a loan would be like dumping cash off a cliff—good money after bad.*

Meanwhile, the everyday citizens and business owners in California have little good to say about how their state is operating, and in fact, they are outraged that the state government continues to raise taxes while refusing to eliminate wasteful spending. Yes, Nero, Rome, played by California in this tragedy, is burning up and down what is now the southern West Coast of the USA. How long will it be until the fire burns itself out?

Many of the big money people throughout the state want California to go out on its own. California should be an independent nation so they say. Brexit gave rise to Calexit and both mean the same. Calexit is looking for a secession path to rid itself of the burden it perceives from being one with the forty-nine other states. Meanwhile, the forty-nine, fearful that California may try to get its debts repaid on their backs favor greasing the skids for the La La Land secession.

After the midterms showed clearly that Democrats still have a lot of voting power in California, the verdict was in. The Golden Bear State was solely responsible for the Democrats winning the House by 38 votes 235D to 197R. There were three vacant seats in the house as we wrote this paragraph.

Out of California's 53 delegates to the House of Representatives, the Democrat caucus in the House collected a majority of 46 to 7 = 39. Consequently, as you can see, the US House Democrat majority comes from the big state of La La Land. Isn't that a great thought? So, if La La Land secedes, guess what? Republicans gain control of the whole country.

Right after the big Dem victory, Hyperloop co-founder and Uber investor Shervin Pishevar, (born March 24, 1974 an Iranian-American entrepreneur, venture capitalist, super angel investor, and philanthropist) announced on election night, via Twitter, that he will help finance a Calexit Leave campaign. He tweeted shortly after, that he will support a "legitimate campaign for California to become its own nation." There are many like-minded big shots in California. Their big money makes their mouths heard. Good riddance to all of you.

It is no secret that California hopes to have the rest of American Taxpayers bail-out its unfunded pension liability, excessive Medicaid and healthcare costs and anything else it can unload for which there is no money in the coffers of Sacramento.

The unfunded pension liability for example is approximately $300 billion and cannot be paid. Yet even this is not a true reflection of the amount taxpayers are ultimately on the hook for, as it assumes unrealistic rates of return on pension investments. When accounting for more realistic rates of return, the unfunded pension liability in the Bear Flag State is closer to $1 trillion.

The national debt is approximately five times the size of the federal budget. California's unfunded pension liability is nearly ten times the size of the state general fund. That's just the unfunded pension liability; the state also has other significant unfunded liabilities with amounts due that would be classified as much higher than Mount Whitney.

Those of us in Pennsylvania not interested in being stiffed by the Gold Coast would take any negatives that come our way from Big Cal disappearing overnight. Let it go. The advantages of no California to Pennsylvania are that great. Even if one day we needed a passport to visit Disneyland, Pebble Beach, the San Diego Zoo, or Alcatraz and Fisherman's Wharf, it would be worth it. Calexit would ensure that taxpayers in the remaining 49 states would not be forced to bail out decades of California profligacy.

The best news about California so far for the rest of the country was Trump's great 2016 victory. It meant at the time that Gov. Moonbeam Brown, Democrats in the California legislature, and the green lobby that funnels cash to them all, would no longer be able to count on the continued promulgation of federal regulations, such as President Obama's doomed Clean Power Plan, to drag other states' economies down with La La Land's.

Calexit would take a big risk off the backs of other American taxpayers in other states. This means in simple terms that California taxpayers would be responsible for the remaining 90% of Medicaid expansion costs which the federal government is supposed to pick up, as well as the 50% of traditional Medicaid that is currently funded by the feds.

Some Californians may want to secede from the U.S. But should they do so, lawmakers in Sacramento would not be humble and play dead. They know they need to significantly raise taxes, cut services, or both in order to fund existing programs—even if they begin to use Pesos.

Since Sacramento always does the wrong thing for California, and secession makes no good sense for the Golden Poppy State, we can almost be assured that Sacramento will press for secession and with all their donor money for advertising and graft, they will get it. That is worthy of a big cheer from the rest of us. Then, the rest is the problem of the Independent Nation of California, whatever name it chooses.

In addition to debt, there are more and more other negatives about La La Land that would no longer be shared with America. For example, as homelessness has been dropping nationwide, it has increased in California. California found a solution for not providing port-a-potties for the homeless by turning the other cheek as more and more bare cheeks let it fly on public streets and sidewalks, parks, and inside buildings. side

Some cities are more infamous in their disregard to sanitary living than others. For example, one of the most beautiful cities in the country (at one time), has turned into a dumping ground for Bay Area bowel movements -- and things have gotten so bad that this California city is now dubbed the "Doo-Doo Capital in the U.S." Californians are not laughing about it and have learned to avoid it using any other method other than going ahead and solving this crisis.

So, as we contemplate whether California should become an independent nation, lawmakers in Sacramento, will add to the misery of Big Cal's citizens who decide to get out of Dodge by more than likely imposing an exit tax, to stem further population hemorrhaging and brain drain. My advice is to get out while you can. It's going down. Hopefully when it makes its complete fall, it will be a state in Mexico.

The flyover crowd wants nothing to do with providing relief from US taxpayers' pocketbooks. Generally speaking, a federal bailout creates bad incentives for elected officials whether they be in California or elsewhere. It's like letting a kid get away with peeing-in-his-pants. Unless, corrected, there will be a lot of urine and the lack of training will bring even more.

Sacramento has always been and still is an unreasonable entity but they always seem to get what they want by hook or by crook. State legislators may be deluded into proposing even larger spending increases in the future, believing that if deficits occur, the US Congress will force taxpayers in other states to pick up the tab. And it would be unfair for sure, in that it would penalize taxpayers in states that have exercised fiscal discipline. Of course, Sacramento cares not an iota about the fiscal hardships it may cause in other states.

In the event the cowards in Congress accede to Sacramento's demands, the federal government would be well within its rights to require fiscal policy changes before offering bailout funds to any state. After all, lenders commonly impose fiscal restrictions on individuals, companies or countries in debt. When the United States offers foreign aid, the grants and loans are often tied to monetary and fiscal policy reforms. The solution demanded by the "Other 49," is no relief. California flaunts its recklessness. Let them live with it. The rest of America did not vote-in the empty suits in Sacramento.

Clearly, the best policy is for Congress to refrain from bailing out any state that gets in trouble. Permission to secede should be granted to California and perhaps other states but the latter should be evaluated on an individual basis. Governors and legislators should not get a free pass from Congress. Instead, they should have to deal with the political fallout from their own reckless spending sprees.

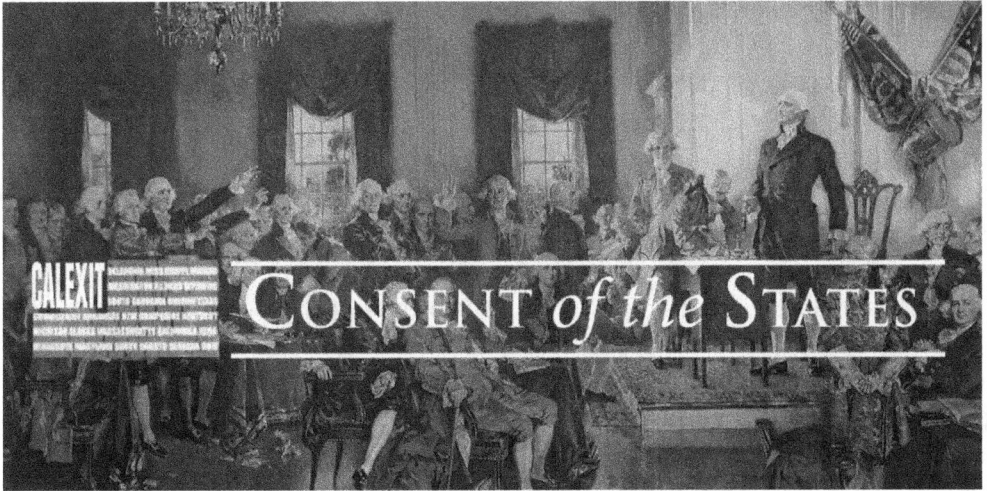

The Supremes say it's OK to secede if…:

There is one easy way to grant California permission to vamoose. *In Texas v. White, the Supreme Court ruled that a state may secede from the Union by either revolution or "through consent of the states". The latter is our ticket (the 49) to freedom from La La Land.*

I surely support the Consent of the States Project; an effort to pass a resolution in a majority of the nation's state legislatures that gives the State of California consent to constitutionally secede from the United States and become an independent country. Let's get on with it. Check out the resolution in the link below and send it once; send it; and send it again. Giving the Big Cal state what it wants is giving the other 49 its best possible deal ever for lots of reasons.

Please propose this resolution in your State legislature:

https://medium.com/@marcus.ruiz.evans/calexit-consent-of-the-states-project-bfb3e2b04c

As beautiful as it is, America and Americans who think just a little about it, soon know that they have to hate California. "It is not just a reaction to California's reaction to Trump, which is over the top. The state is the most hated place in America by Americans—almost the entire time that Barack Obama was the President of America. Check

old newspaper accounts at the library and you will know what we all are now learning. There is no down side for the "*Other 49.*"

Politico writes that just recently-- for the first time—Republicans across America are focusing their hate on California as a whole, instead of individual politicians. They seem to have come to the conclusion that all of California is awful. It wasn't always so. But, perhaps it is now.

Rasmussen polling from March 2017 showed that 41% of Republicans and 32% of all Americans—have no problem at all if California chooses to leave America. This was well before the Sanctuary Cities war of words between Trump and Newsom got hot. Soon it will be over 50% as the Golden State and its uber liberals are annoying the rest of America at an ever-increasing rate.

https://www.politico.com/story/2018/09/13/california-trump-gop-attacks-midterms-818418

Some call the new wave of people *The secessionists*. These activists are funded well and are well tuned into the *Texas v. White* Supreme Court case. They have shifted their focus strategically. They now argue that it will be legal for them to cut ties with the U.S. if a majority of other states agree. They know that Republican-controlled legislatures in the *Other-49* would be happy to push this Democrat-run state right out the nation's front door.

https://reason.com/archives/2018/09/12/if-californians-want-to-secede
To get its way on secession, California needs only to appeal to Republican-controlled state houses across the country. A majority of these would not mind getting rid of a California that is overly dominated by Democrats. Smart thinking would prompt them to be more than willing to give the secession of the La La Land a fair hearing and a positive verdict. Good riddance.

In the other 49-states, as expected the people on the side of California secession are conservatives. Here is a post on California's website.

"Right now, the Republican Party controls the legislatures of 31 states … we need just 25 of them to pass a resolution granting California its consent to exit the Union. And that is our goal and that is what we are working to achieve." Again, good riddance to Big Cal. Good luck with Calexit.

Not funny when it happens to you

Many Republicans lawmakers use California as an example of what happens to states when they're controlled by the Democrats.

No, it is not funny even if some folks such as Sarah Nathan can make an entertaining article out of the new plight of the Hollywood elite. Her tale is true and it is all about Johnny Rotten wanting the cops to stop homeless punks from messing with his life, his wife, and his stuff. Nathan wrote her piece on April 29 after some research on the popular John Lydon, aka Johnny Rotten and his wife Nora Foster

Nobody is spared from the homeless—young or old. **"God save Johnny Rotten!"**

This poor rich guy is enduring anarchy in sunny California, where homeless punks are clearly involved in vandalizing his home.

Sarah Nathan notes that "the former Sex Pistol, punk icon and scourge of the establishment is now appealing to LA cops for help as the unruly young homeless proletariat invade his fancy Venice Beach home."

The one-time mouthpiece of 1977's *Anarchy in the UK*—born John Lydon, took some time to vociferate to Newsweek Reporter, Paula Froelich while being interviewed, to promote the Museum of Arts and Design's new exhibition "Too Fast To Live, Too Young To Die: Punk Graphics, 1976-1986."

John Lydon aka Johnny Rotten and his wife Nora Forster (Inset)

Rotten basically said his life is being made "rotten" by some "rotten" people who do "rotten" things all over LA. Now, they do their things right in his front-yard. He does have compassion but the fact is, as he noted in the interview, the homeless situation in his swanky LA neighborhood has gotten so bad that thieves have been tearing out the protective bars from the windows of his multimillion-dollar home for their scrap value.

They lobby bricks, and then they set up unsightly tent cities in his property and elsewhere and they are constantly littering the beach with syringes. Nobody, whether they have ten dollars in their wallet or ten cents wants to live like that.

Rotten expanded with this missive: "A couple of weeks ago I had a problem. They came over the gate and put their tent inside, right in front of the front door. It's like . . . the audacity. And if you complain, what are you? Oh, one of the establishment elite? No, I'm a bloke that's worked hard for his money and I expect to be able to use my own front door."

Dear suffering Johnny, please give Donald Trump a call and he'll come to help you. Keep nailing him and your buddies of the past will keep nailing you. Do the right thing.

Hey, I am on Rotten's side as *rotten* as it may sound. It is for such reasons that many not-so-well-off as Johnny Rotten are packing it up and leaving the excrement behind while getting out of Dodge. The *Never Mind the Bollocks* hell-raiser added that these unwelcome visitors actually "tried to steal the iron bars off the windows" to sell as scrap metal. It ain't fun if you are living it.

Johnny's wife Nora, battling her own serious issues, "cannot cope" because of all the vicious vagrants in the city. Johnny, take your wife to a nice city. Get out of Dodge.

No, it is not fun in this new LA. Despite the existing trauma, it actually gets worse each day. Johnny added this in his interview: "But at 2 a.m. last week, a brick whizzed through the top floor window, the bedroom. Sorry, Mr. Policeman. I need your help. The vagrants moved in en masse . . . in tent cities. They're all young; they're all like 24. They're aggressive, and because there's an awful lot of them together they're gang-y. And the heroin spikes . . . You can't take anyone to the beach because there's jabs just waiting for young kids to put their feet in — and poo all over the sand."

I don't know Johnny Rotten but nobody deserves to live like this even if at one time or at some-times now, it may still appear a luxurious lifestyle. My advice to Johnny Rotten is to further reinforce your property. Sell it all now for whatever loss you have to take and move someplace that is still nice for you and your wife. Thank God you have the funds and you have not been physically harmed. . Do not tell the fawning press of your new location or they will invite the rabble again to torment you because they are not your friends. God bless you Johnny. Get out of that rotten life ASAP!.

Chapter 2 Few Republicans Have Hope for California

Beautiful Sacramento State Government Offices

Bill McEwen, a writer who most often has the scoop, on May 7, 2018 offered a lot of proclamations for saving California from itself. They say in any place but California, one vote can make all the difference in the world. However, in California there are people and many forces unlike those wielded by the common man. These forces brandish a hundred to a thousand and as much as a billion times the power of the ordinary American. Their definite influence on the California power structure stems from three factors:

- Talent
- Persistence
- Money

Of course, as in most situations in life, money is the root of all evil. In the last election for example, donors gave $1.6 billion to candidates, political committees and parties, according to public records. As big as it is, that whopping total from the 2015-16 cycle did not include funding for federal campaigns and local races such as city councils and county boards. Heaven knows what the final 2018 tally will be but one thing is for sure. The people with the money spend it for the power that it buys. They do not use much of it if any to help with the major poverty and homeless situations throughout the state.

Money does not always go directly to campaigns. There are other ways to buy power. Special interests and other influencers enjoy lobbying public officials with special costly gifts, dinners, and other perquisites. Overall lobbyist spending for the 2017-18 cycle when we collected our info was $341 million. That's why few politicians have not had periods in their terms where they were not well overweight. A lot of the perks come from great, and I mean great dinners.

It is well known that money may not always directly buy you votes, but it can buy you access. "If you have five minutes to make your case to a legislative staffer or two hours to make the case to the legislators themselves, that does not guarantee a win, but it sure tilts the playing field in the lobbyist's direction." Corporations own lobbyists but freelancing lobbyists with access know how to sell their power; and they do—to the highest bidder.

Is it any wonder, after some bills are passed, that the average voter asks, what in the world are these politicians thinking?

It is a very legitimate question. Some lobbyist someplace wanted it done. That is real-power. The legislature is for sale friends, and that is why they must be replaced as often as we can. We the people cannot afford for any politician to get comfortable in office.

No room for Republicans in California

Betsy Mahon, the Chair of the Sacramento Country Republican Party posted an article on New Year's Eve, 2018 titled: *Fear-based Activism is Now Status Quo in the City of Sacramento.* For those from fly-over country like me, it helps to know that Sacramento is the Capitol of California and is the seat of the State government.

She referenced another opinion piece by Sacramento Bee columnist Marcos Bretón, who predicted the absolute demise of Republicans in the City of Sacramento. Mahon still has hope but most Californians and observers from outside the state think there is zero chance the political pendulum will ever swing back to the Republican side.

While Bretón may be correct for the near future, Mahon believes the pendulum does eventually swing the other way, in spite of aggressive tactics currently used to maintain power. I think California is too far gone and Sacramento is part of the problem, not part of the solution.

As of November 29, 2018, there were 39,045 registered Republicans in the City of Sacramento and 68,292 registered with no party preference. While these voters are certainly the minority in the City limits, they don't want to be Democrats but still deserve representation. Deserving and getting are, as we know, two different things.

During the recent election voters in the Sacramento City limits expressed frustration that incumbents were running unchallenged. They were fearful for their children's futures because the school district was failing miserably to manage district finances and educate their students. Low-income renters were hopeless as their leases were not being renewed in favor of recent immigrants whose higher rent was funded by the government.

They complained about being impacted by the increase in crime in their neighborhoods and downtown, and expressed regret that they could not display a bumper sticker or sign in their yard for fear of attracting vandalism. When Democrats control everything, the very perpetrators who are to protect the people, giving them the right to speak against Democrats in a new election, may very well be the Democrats themselves who benefit from the perpetrations.

The people also complained about the police allowing disruption of roadways for political objectives. And, they had no confidence that the sales tax increase would be used to improve any of these concerns.

As the official organization that represents the Republican Party, Mahon noted that one of her tasks was to recruit and support Republican candidates. However, there are a ton of real concerns that prospective candidates must consider before running for office in Sacramento.

As the election approached, for example, voters were receiving a constant barrage of negative media coverage of President Trump's administration. Hard as it is to believe, ahem, the press was the perpetrator and the instigator brining on the negativism. Every Trump tweet was over-analyzed and every bill Trump signed was ignored or distorted using politically motivated headlines.

To maintain sanity, most voters tend to tune out all the negativity and rarely read beyond the headlines. Those who still read the newspaper or listen to news reports are fed a constant stream of doom and gloom coming out of Washington. And, of course it is always blamed on those nasty Republicans.

Protesters aggressively reacted to the shooting of a local man by law enforcement. They went so far as to disrupt City Council meetings (now the norm) and they threatened drivers during commute hours (unimpeded by law enforcement). Those looking for anarchy and hoping to blame it on the Republicans received significant campaign donations from outsiders like George Soros who tried to use the family of the deceased, while mourning the loss of their loved one, to defeat the District Attorney. Sweet, hah?

Local business owners are fed up along with the people. Those who dared to express different opinions relating to current topics on Facebook were shut down by protesters, and their investors and clients caved for fear of their own demise. What a great place to live. America?

Conservative youth groups on college campuses were easy fodder for the bad guys. They were denied their right to free speech and to hear speakers of their choice, while masked protesters burned buildings and attacked those who waved the American flag. Law enforcement took sides but it was not to give help to those harmed.

Conservatives were forced to avoid attending or organizing rallies at the Capitol as they remembered the Trump rally attendees who were violently attacked in San Jose, another once great Cali city after being directed by police into a mob of protesters.

Social media giants gathered and sold the personal data of Republicans that the owners of the data thought was protected, and conservative views were selectively silenced on Facebook and Twitter as they still are to this day. But, the big shots, Mark Zuckerberg (Facebook) and Ev Williams (Twitter) denied any wrong-doing by their companies.

And the always-truthful Democrats had previously proclaimed that this was the year of the woman. Since women are not permitted to have any voice by Republicans (obviously just kidding), the Dems spent hundreds of millions to vilify and defeat Republican women incumbents and candidates up and down the State.

It certainly was not the year of the woman—it was the year to initiate the campaign to defeat President Trump and all that he stands for. Democrats care only about eliminating Trump and folding back the 2016 election to make loser Hillary their queen.

Can we call this fear-based campaigning? Well, if it is not politically incorrect we can. Nonetheless it is fear-based campaigning. It has been working for the current leadership in the City of Sacramento and the State of California. We can ask if it can be sustained. It depends on your time frame. The crooks in Sacramento have been able to get away with it with impunity for quite a long time. So, nothing good is on the horizon. But how about a bright spot right after the horizon?

We know that the history of human civilization shows that fear-based governance doesn't last forever. While it often lasts too long at the expense of many lives lost, eventually, the people rise and new leaders and directions are chosen. Some for the better, some not, but all say they're for the good of their people.

As we see a rise in activism on behalf of socialist policies in Sacramento, San Francisco and Los Angeles, Betsy Mahon wonders if the current leaders know what they're inviting. The activists think they are supporting equality—at least for those who agree with them—while leaders are seeing their policies challenged if they don't produce enough free services, let enough criminals out of jail, or place enough controls on employers (who are fleeing the State in large numbers). It will never be enough if the current leadership continues to appease them so as not to suffer their wrath.

As part of an effort to increase Democrat turnout, the Legislature changed the way we cast our vote. Sacramento County was one of five counties in California to implement a new voting system that replaced polling places with regional vote centers placed around the County strategically to add convenience for urban dwellers who were not known to turn out on election day.

The "Voters Choice Act" also allowed for ballot harvesting and same day registration and voting – no ID required. As a member of the Voters Choice coalition that was organized by the Mayor, Mahon was one of two Republicans who regularly attended meetings. The other 70-100 participants were mostly paid community organizers who were anxious to use this new law to increase Democrat turnout throughout the County.

While the organizers and participants were very cordial to their GOP guests, conversations often were cut short when Mahon joined in. They were unaccustomed to having Republican representation at coalition meetings, and it was very educational for the opposition (Republicans).

What did Republicans learn? They confirmed that they are outspent, out-organized, and have been for a few decades – about the time that Robbie Waters realized he was surrounded by activists who intended to deny every conservative elected and appointed offices.

They don't want diversity—they want to erase independent thought through intimidation. Republicans more and more realize that it takes 100 community organizers working hard through non-profits to convince urban dwellers that their survival depends on well-funded government programs. Republicans also know that the very people who are targeted are potential sympathizers of the Republican approach to issues.

Republicans stand for "opportunity for all." That's different from "free stuff for all." Republicans value people of faith, strong families, rule of law, and entrepreneurial spirit. Republicans believe our country has a right to protect its border and its communities, and we welcome legal immigrants who come here for a better life, not to overturn our way of life.

Contrary to the narrative that billionaire power seekers spread across the internet, our platform is not racist, homophobic, misogynistic or hateful. "Opportunity for all" has been misinterpreted successfully by well-funded messengers, and that is where we must focus our comeback.

So why would a Republican ever want to run in a City whose leaders tolerate and benefit from fear-based political activism? Is it right that a business owner, non-profit leader, or person of faith has to jeopardize their family, their safety, or their livelihood to run for office under the banner that supports their morals and outlook for equal opportunity?

Betsy Mahon does not think so nor do values-oriented Republicans, who together will continue to support the brave souls who stand up to represent the minority of GOP voters in the City of Sacramento—who deserve to be heard.

Republicans have a lot to offer the City of Sacramento and the State of California. Whether the concern is the increase in poverty and homelessness due to the high cost of living, the dismal record of achievement in our public schools, crime in our communities, or billions of dollars of unfunded pensions, we have a different approach that should be considered by leadership.

Republicans openly challenge Democrat politicians who control the cities and State of California to acknowledge the issues that matter to the average voter, and to care more for solutions than power.

The people would be better served through inclusion of diverse ideas. No need to fear though there may be reason to fear. Nobody is calling for a real fight but that may be what ultimately resolves the conflict.

Politics won't get any better for Californians with Calexit other than those who make the escape and flee to other states before the break. Having the same leaders in an independent country for today's Californians won't change anything.

Golden State loses its luster

California is a state that has always had a certain luster.

Since the discovery of gold at Sutter's Creek in 1849, California has been a dream destination. Only recently have many people from the flyover states and poor East Coast States such as Pennsylvania decided there are better places to walk than the feces-strewn pathways with drug paraphernalia and the finest wastes a body can create in a quick hide-and seek dump. And, so the flyover crowd no longer picks feces-strewn California as a favorite vacation destination.

The folks in the middle of America can get sights and sounds and smells like that in public restrooms. No need to travel to California for such a treat.

I admit, for the longest many years from 1974 onward 'til about ten to twenty years ago, I would take a free trip to California from IBM in a heartbeat and often did. It was actually part of my job. I loved the State…but things have changed.

Chapter 3 California Was a Wow for Me!

Great Conventions and Great Vacations

In my fourth year with IBM, at 25-years old, the company honored me with my first Systems Engineering Symposium. This was a major award consisting of a free trip to a great place (San Francisco), access to the best IBM speakers, and access to the best motivational speakers of the era such as Richie Ashburn, Merlin Olson, Walter Cronkite, Henry Kissinger, and many others.

IBM spared no expense on cocktail hours with minimal alcohol but the finest red & white wines to go along with massive hors d'oeuvres and the piece de resistance—row boats full of iced fresh shrimp, crabmeat claws, clams, oysters, etc. I gain weight just thinking of my massive overindulgence at such events.

This exquisite 1974 happening occurred on the first day of the conference and was so well done, that my buddy Dennis Grimes and I, from the same IBM office, decided to do it one more time on the Q T. We rigged the system by staying for the afternoon greeting cocktail hour for the second group.

IBM had brought our group in from Monday to Wednesday and then another group from Wednesday to Friday. The crab-claws and the lobster sized shrimp were so appealing that Dennis and I used our beginning of the Conference badges for the second-round stuff-fest and then we took off to see the rest of California. It worked.

IBM always found the best entertainment possible for a special evening during the conference. I can recall the late Andy Gibb, The Beach Boys when in their prime, Frankie Valli, who is always great, and other stars, wooing the young folks at these IBM extravaganzas. Every IBM person in the world wanted to get their own personal invitation to these events.

They had IBM names such as The Golden Circle, the Hundred Percent Club, The IBM Means Service Group or the IBM Systems Engineering Symposium. It made working hard for IBM seem like it was worth it. At the time, it sure was. After one Symposium, I know that I could not wait to earn another.

IBM picked California the most often as the event site though most of its labs and headquarter operations were in the Northeast. Perhaps because of that, the employees loved a March trip to California to get out of the glum dullness and the cold of the Northeast. The treat began landing in the beautiful garden look of California with its warmth, and its historic cities and sites and pleasantries.

I had the pleasure of being invited to a number of these events by working harder than I might have otherwise worked. They were mostly held in California cities such as San Francisco, San Diego, Los Angeles, and Anaheim. Thank you, IBM.

Additionally, a number of IBM education facilities were in San Francisco and other areas of California and a side benefit of going to a five-day school was the weather and the overstay factor, which was often the following weekend or longer. IBM of course. paid only for the time we spent at the education center.

A major IBM users group known as COMMON often chose cities in California as the spot for its semi-annual computer education weeks and expositions. My clients at IBM in Scranton PA insisted that I accompany them to these grand events and of course my wife would accompany me. These were fantastic and all-expenses were paid by IBM on behalf of my customers.

I never knew how being part of IBM could educate me. I like to say that I joined IBM and I saw the world. That's the truth. I always knew that if I did not do my job, life at Big Blues would not be easy.

San Francisco was Phenomenal

My first Systems Engineering Symposium was in San Francisco at the St. Francis Hotel. IBM got us all rooms at the St. Francis. IBM had a policy that IBMers from different cities and states would be joined with IBMers from other cities and states at registration. None of us at such a great event were inclined to complain about a roommate though nobody liked it. Nonetheless, the rest of the events were first class.

To save a few bucks for Big Blue, we were all forced to meet a new person and sleep in the same room with them for three days to a week. Snoring was not a major offense and getting a solo room facing the IBM gendarme was almost never a possibility. One feared that a complaint on accommodations would affect one's ability to selected for excellence the next year.

But, if you were bringing your wife, as I did this first year, it was not easy. Theoretically, IBM had no opinion about whether you did or did not bring a spouse. If you let it be known, they would not bunk you with somebody else but then you then had to pay half of your room fee as the fee for your wife or husband.

At my first Symposium, I paid for my wife as did the other Systems Engineer from our office, Carmen P. who accompanied me. We stayed in the older part of the St. Francis which was quite elegant and the experience was very enjoyable.

The SF Cable Car Line stopped right in front of the St. Francis Hotel. How fortunate. We got on often and went on both cable car routes. We would wind up either at the Buena Vista Coffee House which served the first Irish Coffee in San Francisco or we went right to Fisherman's Wharf. You too would smile on either route.

We were amazed at the beauty of San Francisco at the time. Carmen and I loved beer also and so we took the Cable Car, found a few beers at the wharf, and found something we talk about to this day. On the street

corners at the time, we could get a Dixie cup full of shrimp, prawns, squid, or crabmeat for not much more than 50 cents. We washed all the sea food down with Coors beer, a Colorado-brew that could not be bought on the East Coast at the time.

We liked the Dixie cups very much and yes, even more so than the beer. Whenever were in the rental car heading for the Golden Gate Bridge, we would trek by the Wharf and would stop briefly in the congestion at various corners. One of our number would get out quickly and bring back the loot consisting of multiple Dixie cups of some great sea food. Sometimes we would go around the block a few times just to get more.

On one day, Carmen and I, while the ladies were shopping, took off for Coit Tower on a walking tour. We made it. What a great experience overlooking San Francisco and the Bay.

Note Coit Tower Has a look like a Fire Hose Nozzle

On the way, we found a haunt called Guido's where we quenched our thirsts with, what else—beer. Before we came home from this trip, Carmen had permitted me to nickname him Guido. I am afraid to this day as we remain great friends, whether he is OK with the nickname. He's a great guy.

Name a place. We were there and it was great. And there were no drug needles and no fecal waste in 1974 in San Francisco.

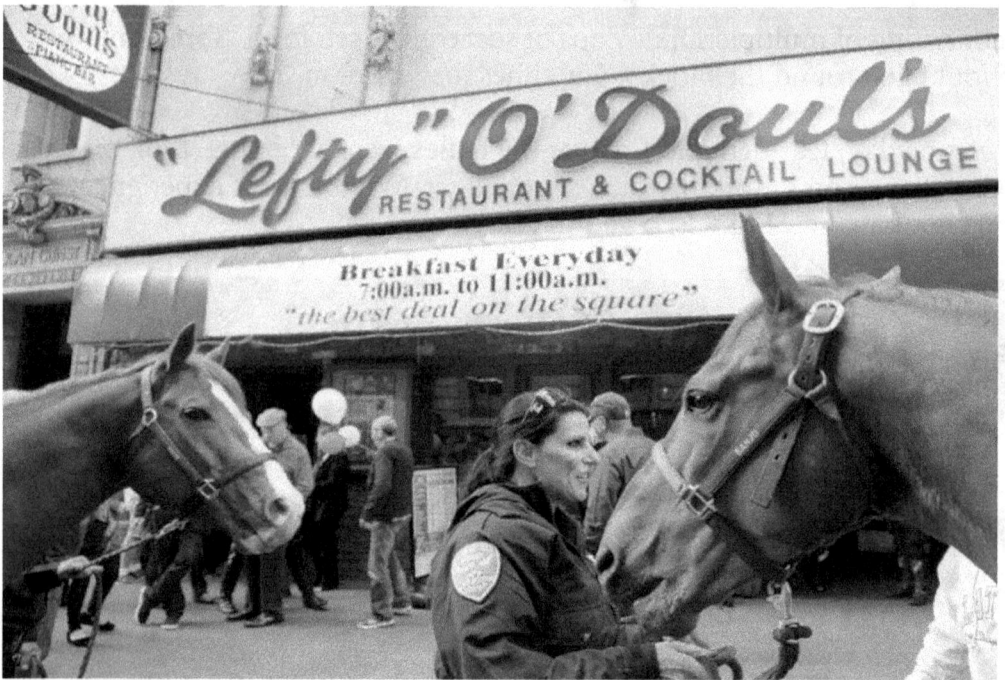

We went to Ghirardelli Square and had the finest chocolates and we had dinner at a Mexican Smorgasbord place at the Cannery and we found other great local spots such as Lefty O'Douls at Union Square (Recently moved to the Wharf).

It was a vacation like one could not possibly get in Northeastern PA. Before we took off for Denver, we drove to the Napa Valley and did our share of wine tasting at all the great spots. It was like living in another world. Nothing in California was unsightly. It was to die for.

We left for Denver and that is another great story about the great big trees (Sequoias) as it took a few days to get there. We stayed in a Holiday Inn just outside of Mile High Stadium, where the Denver Broncos played.

California was so nice at the time, we could not wait to get back

Other Trips to California

I came back to Pennsylvania from California wondering why everybody did not live there. Eventually, my buddy Guido moved across the Bay from San Francisco for years and he took the Ferry Boat to work every day. He loved it. My wife and I took our kids some years later to San Francisco and Anaheim for Disneyland and while in San Francisco, we visited Guido and his new bride on one of our trips when we had the kids with us.

I think we stayed in the St Francis and the kids loved it. My kids are very smart and they noticed that all was not well in San Francisco. Wherever we went, there were panhandlers in the streets, especially at the Cable stops. It spooked the kids and it spooked us too. We hoped then, twenty-five years ago that SF officials would eventually solve the problem so we could go back to a better city. They did not address the problem so we did not ever go back as a family.

The kids loved Anaheim & Disneyland. So did we.

We loved the old original Disneyland Hotel in Anaheim. When the City gave up some streets for Disney to expand, the Disneyland Hotel, which I remembered, disappeared. Yes, in the picture on the next page, that is the red MonoRail on the second floor of the old--and for me—the always graceful Disneyland Hotel. Its new incarnation cannot even come close to mimicking its older charm with the great western line dances every night . Not everything gets better with change.

Disneyland is in Anaheim, which is in Orange County, California. It is still a great place to go but the fact is all of California is falling apart. Orange County stands as an outlier in California, a state that has become increasingly friendly to illegal immigrants.

At a time when state leaders resisted President Trump's hard line against illegal immigration, Orange County Sheriff Sandra Hutchens reached out to the Trump administration, stating that she wanted her deputies to work more closely with federal immigration officials

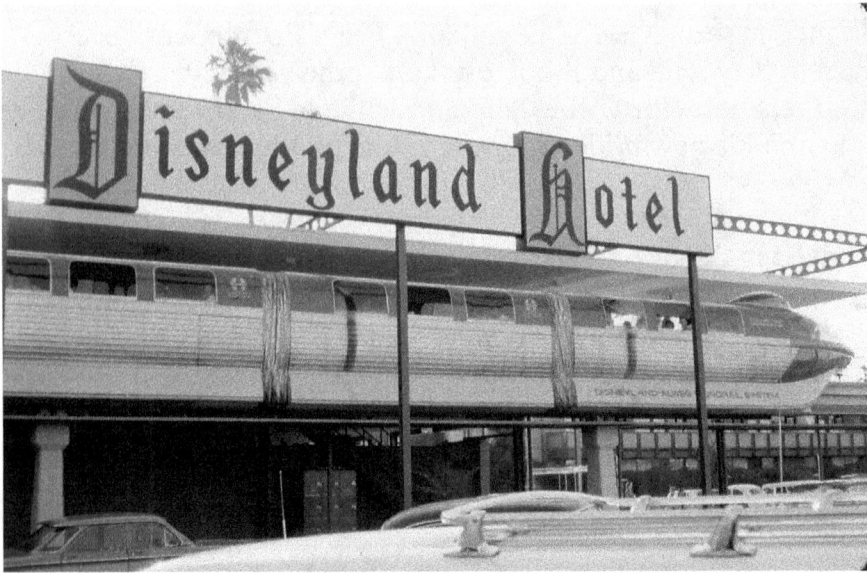

When state legislators drafted Senate Bill 54, a measure that positioned the Golden State as a "sanctuary" for those who are in the country without legal status, Hutchens vehemently spoke out in opposition.

But as 2017 drew to a close and with SB 54 taking effect at the start of this year, Hutchens took a step back and ended her agency's participation in a federal-local immigration enforcement program known as 287(g), which allowed Orange County deputies to act as immigration agents in its jail.

There is a lot of pressure on all officials in California to toe the line with the dictators in this dictator state. They say the Brown, Pelosi, Getty, and Newsom families run the show. Nobody named Reagan would ever get elected today.

Hutchens felt compelled to announce she'd halt her department's participation in program because it would run afoul of the state legislation that she'd lobbied against but was ultimately signed into law by Gov. Jerry Brown in October. Still, Hutchens promised to cooperate with ICE as much as the law allowed. Orange County, for example, has a contract to house ICE detainees in its two jails and will continue to do so.

Orange County was the last bastion of reasonableness in a state that ought to wall itself off from the rest of the country and rip down its wall at the Mexican border.

It was a long time for me to go back to California – maybe 25 years. The second-last time we went way west was to La Jolla by the Sea and it was pleasant and the next time was Northern Lake Tahoe which is very affluent. Neither of these areas seemed to me much affected by the needles and pins and the feces. We were there for a wedding and it could have been in the northeast as there were no issues for us at all—but having been to CA before, we were not trusting. My advice is to trust in certain areas of the state, but verify and verify and verify.

We stayed about a half-hour from South Lake Tahoe where the Casinos are. Here is a picture of South Lake Tahoe that captures the magnificence of the area. It is still beautiful as of 2018. Yes, I would recommend it if you are headed to California. By the way, half of Lake Tahoe is in Nevada, where there is gambling if you like it.

Casinos in South Lake Tahoe with great view of the lake & mountain peaks

Chapter 4 Is the Gold Rusting in the Golden State?

A San Bernardino County firetruck plunged off Interstate 15, when a lane and shoulder caved in due to heavy rains in the Cajon Pass on Feb. 18. IRFAN KHAN *LOS ANGELES TIMES*

Those who today write about the Golden State see the fracturing of the old and the replacement of the old with "sh**." Sorry for the crass effect of that word but that is the whole truth. Still, most dignified writing attempts to purify the wording by labeling it feces. The meaning, however, remains the same.

Everywhere you turn, there are big problems that California leaders for many years seem disinterested in solving. Look at the picture above in which an entire lane disappeared swallowing up a Fire Truck. Even if politicians wanted to solve the problems and even tried a little; their efforts failed.

Californians will tell you that unlike the golden days, their roads are crumbling. Their schools are failing. Homelessness is skyrocketing. Farmers go without water while fish and wildlife remain endangered. The goofs in charge remain goofs and continue to be reelected. The dictatorship is like all others. It has lost its ability to function. People are leaving in droves.

Meanwhile, the state has been spending billions every year on a high-speed rail system that might not ever be completed and it's been so long this way that its underlying technology may soon be outdated before the system is even on-line. Just recently, the state decommitted on parts of the railway. It's not that that is a bad idea. It's that when Democrats begin to control anything, it is the beginning of a short trip to the boneyard.

Recently an email has been circulating that shows the success of a reputable rebuilding program of Hiroshima Japan over the 65 years since the bomb dropped. It compares this with the effects of Democrat leadership in Detroit over the same period. It helps to recall that Detroit was once a bustling, booming metropolis as the biggest car-building city in the world. With Democrat leadership in California, am I saying that the Golden State is on its way to being another Detroit. The answer to that is an emphatic, YES!

Hiroshima 65 years after the bomb

Detroit 65 years after the bomb

Building Blocks of Poverty

Once a prosperous state just like Michigan, California is nothing like its glorious past. Nearly 70 percent of poor Californians spend more than half of their income on rent. No wonder they are fleeing to nearby states.

According to a McKinsey Global Institute report, California needs 3.5 million more homes than it has now. That's why home purchases and home rentals are so high.

Somebody might ask why the Democrats in Sacramento (State capital) were not watching and coming up with ideas long ago on how to keep pace with the population explosion – mostly illegal.

One would conclude with no other information, that California—the home of to Silicon Valley and some of the world's brightest minds and highest salaries—would be on the cutting edge of everything including education. It is not. It is lagging. K-12 education is controlled by the California Teachers Association, which is most concerned about negotiating wages and benefits for its members. A quality education is an after-thought.

California's leaders are all members of the Democratic Party and that is a fact. Democrats of yore stuck up for the little guy. No longer. The big shots mostly ignore the plight of the citizens and non-citizens alike and instead brag about having the world's sixth-largest economy. Even at that size, it is not doing well by its people.

Democrat leaders do not like to mention some embarrassing facts such as California having more poor people (by percentage and total number) than any other state in America when you factor in its outlandish cost of living. Nearly 21% of Californians live in abject poverty.

Florida by the way was approaching the second-highest poverty rate but those days are long gone. The Sunshine State over the last few years is much, much better—moving from 17% to 14%. Why? Democrats do not control Florida. Florida's poverty rate peaked in 2012 at 17.1 percent. While things have improved to the current 14 percent figure, it is still higher than the national rate of 13.2 percent but nowhere close to the runaway numbers (21%) for California

Leadership is always the problem. Giveaway Democrats soon run out of money, raise taxes to the roof, and then the people become poor and many begin heading to other states where they can survive.

So, who has been killing California?

There are many articles though no great expose's on how four families—Brown, Newsom, Getty, and Pelosi control everything worth anything in California. I have also seen what is called the Baker's Dozen of California's Movers, Shakers and Blockers. This too is very insightful.

The bottom line is they are all Democrats and they care little for their state other than as it affects their own pocketbooks.

(1) Gov. Jerry Brown now Gov. Gavin Newsom top the power list. Note the last names. Recently, columnist Joe Mathews opined that California's governorship had amassed so much power that it ranked second in the nation to the occupant of the White House.

(2) California Teachers Association
The teachers' union describes itself as "one of the strongest advocates for educators in the country." It co-sponsors legislation and endorses political candidates. Its political war chest, funded by the contributions of its 325,000 members, rewards friends and punishes enemies. It runs education in the state—not the government. The CTA unfailingly opposes changes to a teacher tenure system that provides lifetime job protections after the first 24 months. Elsewhere in the country, students are better protected from ineffective teachers by laws that grant tenure after three to five years of teaching.

(3) Robbie Hunter. Most of us in fly-over country have never heard of him. But everyone in Sacramento knows the face and name of the president of the 400,000-member State Building and Construction Trades Council. Hunter is a staunch supporter of prevailing wage laws and project labor agreements. Here's what he wrote in response to critics last year in a Los Angeles Daily News op-ed: "The idea behind the prevailing wage is to keep unscrupulous operators from low-bidding the legitimate competition to the detriment of the local workforce. The effect has been to allow blue-collar workers ... to maintain their place in the American middle class." His organization bankrolled enough political campaigns for this master at the game to be the most powerful figure in the state.

(4) SEIU. The Service Employees International Union represents public employees, health-care workers and blue-collar employees in food service, security and maintenance. It has 700,000 members in California, and is a huge force in elections and making or breaking proposed laws. It spends a ton of members money each election cycle, and Democratic candidates compete for its endorsement. Republicans have no chance.

(5) Metropolitan Water District. This political force is governed by a 38-member board. It procures the water that ultimately flows to 19 million people in southern California. How big is MWD? It has resources to change what would be lost government projects such as Gov. Brown's Delta tunnels project by donating billions to preserve the project.

agreeing to finance Much of California's future will be written by those who control water. MWD is the 800-pound gorilla of H20, and its influence will only grow if the tunnels clear environmental hurdles to become reality. The future prosperity of California hinges on water availability. With Metropolitan going all in on the tunnels, it will have a big say in how much southern California residents and water-starved farmers south of the Delta pay for water.

(6) Mary Nichols. Who is she? A 'rock star' of influence as the top air quality regulator." She served Gov. Brown as the head of the California Air Resources Board from 1979 to 1983 and then returned as the state's air-pollution czar in 2007.

The NY Times says she is the de facto enforcer of the single biggest step the United States has taken to combat the effects of climate change. ... " She is a new Green Deal kind of person. In other words, she wants more people to give up their cars and take mass transit.

(7) Xavier Becerra. He is the successor appointed by Brown to the state attorney general post when Kamala Harris left mid-term for the U.S. Senate. Becerra is the face of liberal "resistance" to the Trump administration's positions on immigration and the environment and law enforcement. Yes, he is the state's top law enforcement official. His hand is in virtually everything.

There are more individuals and many more entities in California who wield great power. California is a huge state and to remind us all it would be a large country if it were not attached to the US. Perhaps if it could be rejoined with the Baja section and again be part of Mexico, it would be better for America. We'll talk more about this for sure in this book. Hasta La Vista California!

We've all heard the notion that "as California goes, so goes the nation." Most of us our here in fly-over country are hoping tht maxim goes away as I would not wish California on anybody. It is such a shame what is happening to that once great state. Once the veritable epicenter of the American Dream, the only valid California Dream today is to get the H___ out.

Man is destroying California with bad laws and a lack of concern for real American values. Most of the good of California continues to exist featuring some of the most beautiful natural landscapes in the entire world. The state has gorgeous weather and it once had a booming economy. Now, people are moving out of the state by the millions because life in California has literally become a nightmare for so many people. The cause of the demise of this once great state is that too many buffoons operate out of Sacramento.

I have nothing against the state personally. I always loved my visits but the caretakers have presided over the rotting of the state. Mostly everybody whoever visited California twenty or more years ago dreamt of eventually getting their own place on the coast. Now even those for whom California was once number one would not be able to handle being stuck there for more than a few days. Being in California for anybody is no longer advisable.

Many of those who live in California today with choices are thinking of how to find a way to move out of the state. There are far too many reasons why you shouldn't live in California and few reasons why you should stay. A trip to San Francisco is all it would take today for you to know why. Soon the rest of the state will join the cesspool.

Sixteen reasons not to live in California

Tyler Durden of Zerohedge found sixteen reasons for human beings not to live anywhere in California. Let's look at some of his reasons mixed in with mine below:

1. Besides excrement and drug needles, there is one big fault called The San Andreas Fault. Researchers with the U.S. Geological Survey released

the results of the years-long study warning a major earthquake could strike soon. Who needs that?

2. Studies show that out of all 50 states, the state of California has been ranked as the worst state for business for 12 years in a row. 513 CEOs from across the nation ranked California 50th in taxation and regulation, 35th in workforce quality and 26th in living environment, which includes cost of living, the education system and state and local attitudes toward business. Notably, California placed worst among the nine states in the Western region in all three categories. Blame Sacramento.

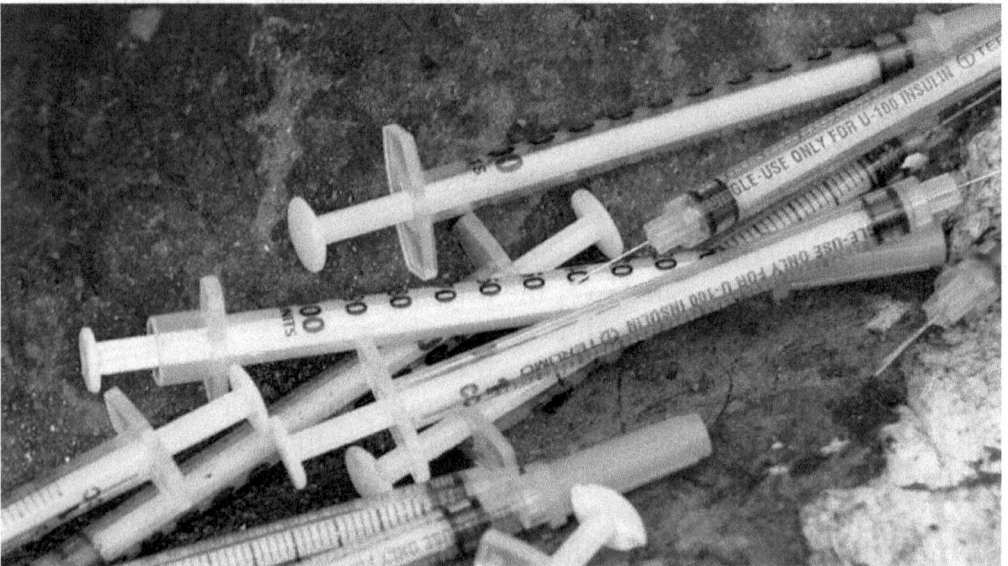

San Francisco bans plastic straws but drug needles can be tossed with impunity

3. Who wants the highest state income tax rates in the entire nation? Move to Texas and buy a new car every year with the tax difference.

4. The Democrat leaders in Sacramento are insane and they are getting worse not better. The state government in Sacramento seems to go a little bit battier with each passing session. You cannot trust they will ever do the right thing. Thus, prospects for a better life are nil without moving out of Dodge.

5. Los Angeles is reported to now have the worst traffic in the entire world, and San Francisco is not far behind.

6. The tons of money being made in Silicon Valley for now at least does not make up for the exploding poverty rate in the state. Before Newsom, L.A. City Council recently asked Governor Jerry Brown "to declare homelessness a statewide emergency."

7. With unchecked illegal immigration, crime is on the rise in many California cities. The Mexican drug war, raging for years south of the border, spilling into the state. Many leave the state for that reason alone.

Sanctuary city status at fault for CA murder suspect being on the loose

Everybody is suing everybody else in the state and out of the state. California is one of the most litigious states in the entire nation. California is ranked 47th out of all 50 states.

9. Every year wildfires and mudslides wreak havoc in the state. Erosion is particularly bad along the coast. The California coastline are literally falling into the ocean.

10. California housing prices are ridiculous. There is a documented case in San Francisco in which a struggling engineer was paying $1,400 a month to live in a closet.

11. Key infrastructure elements of California are falling to pieces.

12. Though 5355 miles away, radiation from the ongoing Fukushima nuclear disaster continue to cross the ocean and wash up along the California coastline.

13. Illegal drug use in the state is at epidemic proportions. Users shoot up in front of kids on city streets. Emergency rooms are being flooded by heroin overdose victims.

14. There are reports that Russia is "quietly 'seeding' the U.S. shoreline with nuclear 'mole' missiles." Everything that is outrageous in past thinking is now reality so there are few reasons to believe this is not happening.

15. North Korea cannot be dismissed as a major nuclear threat as well. It is being reported that the North Koreans are developing an ICBM that could potentially reach the west coast of the United States...

16. Do you think that it is still possible that a very large earthquake will produce a major tsunami on the west coast? The LA Times has reported one study which found that a magnitude 9.0 earthquake along the Cascadia fault could potentially produce a massive tsunami that would "wash away coastal towns. At least Lex Luther has not begun to purchase land in Nevada hoping to have west coast property soon.

Estimates are that over the past decade, approximately five million people have moved away from California. If these are government figures and since governments always try to whitewash statistics, it may very well be fifteen million.

In 2019, unfortunately the promise of the Golden State has been long shattered. We have documented that already there is a mass exodus out of the state as families flee the horrific nightmare that California has become and the fact that there are no solutions coming with Democrats still 100% in control.

Chapter 5 Should the Other 49 States Let California Secede?

Yes!!! Boy does that sound good!

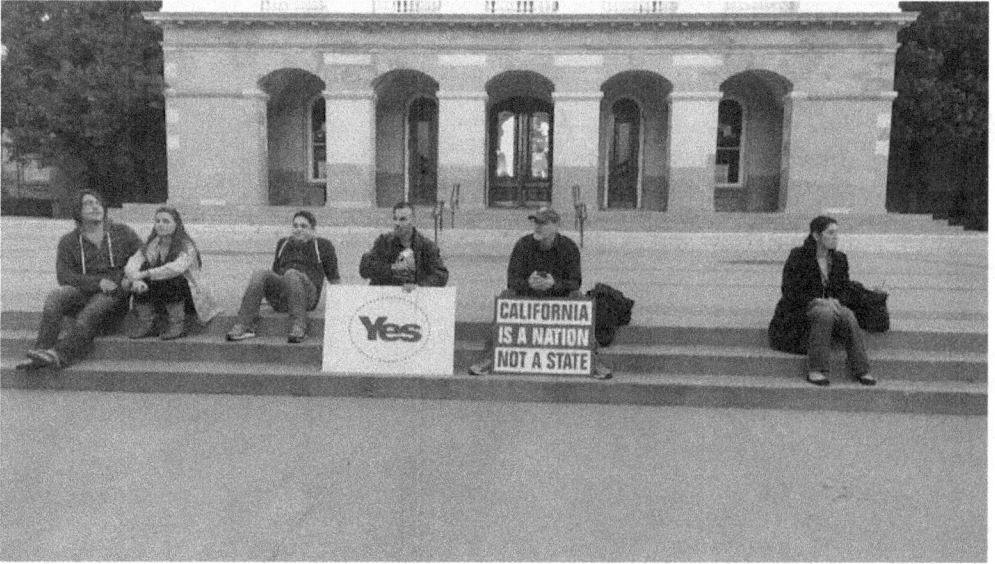

In 2008, those of us with strong recollections do recall that the fake news media tried its darndest to conceal it when Obama said he had visited just about all of the **57** states. Can you imagine if Trump had said that? Most of us know that there are 50 states regardless of the opinion of a past president.

Watching California thumb its nose to the rest of the country for years with sanctuary cities and now being a sanctuary state and by amassing huge deficits and then looking for relief on the backs of US taxpayers for too many years, I know that I thought often about how nice it would be to have just 49 states. Why not let California do its own thing? It is OK with me.

Now I am seeing articles about the move for California to secede from the United States (the so-called "Calexit"). Well, the more I think about it, I am convinced that a vote to split is inevitable rather than improbable. Will groups such as the California Freedom Coalition succeed in getting enough signatures each election cycle that one day secession will be on the ballot and then on another day, it will pass?

You may know that it is very easy to get an initiative on the ballot in California. Those taking odds believe that passage of a secession referendum–even secession itself–might be tough but it would not be impossible. If I have a right to speak on behalf of the rest of the country, "Dear California, I would offer this comment: Hasta La Vista California. Yes indeed, Hasta La Vista, Baby!"

Regular people in regular states are simply sick of California's incessant whining and bullying and its bull-crap. The state already has an easily abused ballot system and its politics are vastly out of sync with the rest of America. Besides that, don't we all think that California is a little full of itself.

You see. California isn't like New York City, which—while it's the economic and cultural center of basically the world—realizes that it needs the rest of the country for food, water, power, and a place to send its garbage. (New York's annual garbage haul? 7.8 million tons per year. Where are you going to put that when you can't even find a parking space in Queens?)

California is off on solo flights all the time and has no time to even perceive that it needs anyone, and massive ego is annoying to most of us. The state may be enormous in terms of geography, population, economy, and very importantly its coastline. It always was a great state and its agricultural base could sustain the state by itself.

With a country full of Trump for the good, California as a state does not like the President of the United States. Some have concluded that with its high Latino population, California particularly does not appreciate Trump's rhetoric about the "wall with Mexico."

The rest of us of course would be OK with a nice peaceful secession and border walls built on the Eastern Side of California in Nevada and Arizona. Then, none of us would care at all about the California / Mexico border. In fact, Maybe California can join Mexico as one of its states.

So let's assume for a moment that California leaves, and when it does, the following five things would happen quickly:

1. There will be no more California

It would be easy to simply make the state part of Mexico, but the whiners would complain and so that would probably not happen. Instead, Californians would devise a goofy plan to split up the state into a number of parts and the big moose state as we know it would cease to exist.

The first burg to split off would be Silicon Valley. They say it would form want to stay independent of the rest of New California. It would be its own independent, Luxembourg-like nation, where it can ignore international law and avoid paying taxes.

There have long been plans to divide California in two such as West VA and Virginia. Let them do what they want. I don't care as long as California goes away. There might be some Eastern parts of California that would want to stay attached to the mainland US. That would complicate things but might be able to be accommodated

Also, much of California, such as the Northeast portion will want to stay in America. Note this election night infographic from The New York Times.

Geographically, it looks like about half of California is red. Hmm. There would be a lot of questions such as what the loss of that land mass would do to the state's self-sustaining agriculture?

Split it up via Republican / Democrat 2016 totals.

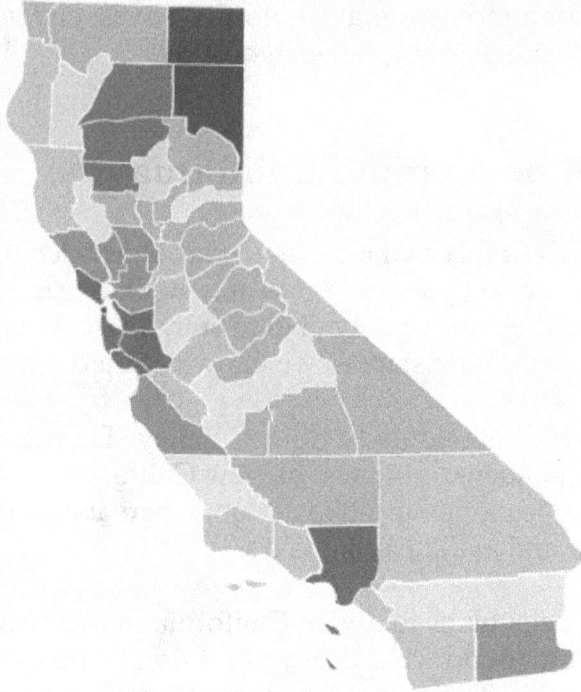

County results

Clinton: ▨ 40–50% ▨ 50–60% ▨ 60–70% ▨ 70–80% ▨ 80–90%
Trump: ▨ 40–50% ▨ 50–60% ▨ 60–70% ▨ 70–80%

Check 'em out to see which part goes/stays

2. New California would suspend long-standing liberties.

Modern day progressivism would rule the day. So the rule would be a mixture of anarchy and fascism. You know that even today's California wants to control your sugar consumption while de-criminalizing every dangerous drug available. That's how it would be with Sacramento in charge.

California has little love for First Amendment freedoms—except the right to protest. So, there would not be a lot of freedom of speech, religion, or even the press in New California. Those rights get in the way of thought-policing and lawsuits. California already has more lawyers than it need so I hope they don't get to move to "America." Californians will need to sue to stay in business so the lawyers can eat.

3. Old benefits not assured in New California

Like most states, today California benefits enormously from its membership in our fraternity of states. Without influence in D.C., California will have to renegotiate its benefits from their new federal government. They would have to pay for military protection to the US or fire up their own army and navy.

Ironically if California recruits are needed for their new armed services contingents, it helps to remember that the Golden State has one of the lowest rates for providing military enlistees, so there might be an even bigger problem there. California may need a draft to survive. Water will also become an issue.

With the Colorado River not flowing outward from California but inward from other states, control is gone. Water may be a big problem. New California will have to pay to get water where today in Washington the California Delegation is so big, they overwhelm all the other Western states in Congress. How are they going to water for their life-saving marijuana farms if Colorado, Utah, and others pull the plug on the water going into the state.

4. New California will fail as independent state

California became an industrial power through capitalism, not progressivism. They have forgotten how to be capitalists. Its accumulated advantages are decades and even centuries old, whether it's from higher education, the military industrial complex that birthed Silicon Valley, the great coastline, or even just the nice weather. It would be almost impossible to ruin a place with California's advantages.

However, the important officials in Sacramento are already doing their best to try.

Were California to kick the few remaining grown-ups out of the room, there would be no one left to keep the state on track.
Will National Republicans in Washington help New California, the Country or will they have to learn to swim themselves?

5. Republicans will control Washington forever.

Without California as a state, Republicans will run Washington forever if California goes away through secession. California is the only thing keeping the Democratic Party relevant on the national scale. Republicans have won every run-off race in 2017 and just picked up another governor. The Democratic Party is in shambles. It is in shambles in the California of today also but still in charge.

If it were not for California, Trump would have won the popular vote by almost 1.5 million. Most importantly, without the California Congressional caucus in Washington, the Republican edge in the House of Representatives almost doubles.

The Democrats would lose two Senate seats too, which isn't as significant, but if a Red California talks Sacramento into letting it stay with the union of 49 states, that would be a four-seat swing. Boom! Boom! Boom!

Secession did not work last time because it was a moral issue. The last time anyone tried something like this, the central issue was slavery and the brutal Civil War ensued, still the deadliest of all America's conflicts.

But California annoys all states and most non-Democrats. So, a fight to preserve the union more than likely would not happen this time. So, many hope again in a few years that California voters decide to divorce the rest of America. The other states would surely do well in the custody battles.

There are many signs much of the rest of America would cheerfully let California go, just to get rid of them. Perhaps the most significant of those indications takes the form of a lawsuit that essentially says California has gotten too big for its britches. It has and it is way to heavy for the rest of the union to carry.

This isn't about California's lousy lifestyle choices, Hollywood and limousine liberals, or its "resistance" to President Trump's administration and its edicts, even though he became president over the strong opposition of most California voters. What is it then?

California is flouting the limits federal law puts on California's regulatory reach. As one of fifty states, California lacks federal power to regulate agriculture or commerce beyond its state borders but it does not seem to care. California is enacting law after law governing other states' economies," says the action, filed in the Ninth Circuit Court of Appeals by those states that would be pleased to se Cal-Exit work better than Brexit.

The other states don't like California's Global Warming Solutions Act of 2006, aiming to cut greenhouse gas emissions to 1990 levels by 2020. "This standard makes businesses that sell fuels in California reduce the carbon intensity of their fuels by 10 percent. This is an actual gripe by a friend of the court filed in a brief submitted by the state of Missouri. Essentially, the bill severely cut use of out-of-state ethanol in gasoline, seriously impacting Iowa and other corn-producing states. It is not good to fool with the economies of other states.

Objecting states also worry that California may start a contagion affecting their businesses negatively. "Worse still," their brief adds, "other states like Massachusetts and Colorado have begun to follow California's lead and pass extraterritorial laws themselves." One of the reasons the 13 Colonies formed the union was for mutual strength but it prohibited any strong state from waging war—any kind of war, on a neighboring state.

Getting rid of California may happen before California divorces the US

Too many regular people in flyover country are interested in cutting California off the US map to think this issue will go away just because Californians may have second thoughts. The Secession of California to more than one would have ever imagined, is now seen as a positive step for America.

Present-day California at one time formed part of the Mexican province of Alta California until the outbreak of the Mexican-American War in May 1846. The next month, 30 American settlers seized a Mexican garrison in Sonoma and declared an independent republic. An updated form of their flag, emblazoned "California Republic," is currently the flag of California..

The republic never performed any administrative functions as a government and lasted less than a month before U.S. Navy Lieutenant Joseph Revere landed at Sonoma and raised a Union flag. So, California became part of the Union before it had a chance to be an independent state.

Present-day arguments for California sovereignty center on the state's large population and economic power. At $2.46 trillion in 2015, California's gross domestic product (GDP) was larger than France's ($2.42 trillion). Using World Bank figures, California would be the world's fifth or sixth largest economy, if it were an independent country. Today it is approaching #5.

California was home to 40.02 million people in April 2019, according to the Census Bureau, slightly more than Uganda; as an independent country, it would be the world's 36th most populous if it were able to secede intact. Cultural issues, while more muted, have featured in independence rhetoric, particular as they relate to environmental issues.

The great irony of Calexit is that these people's solution to Trump's imposing a political border (between the U.S. and Mexico) is to create another political border—between California and New California. I admit I like the solution as do many others sick of Democrat bullies in California.

Chapter 6 Will Democrats Choose the California Wall?

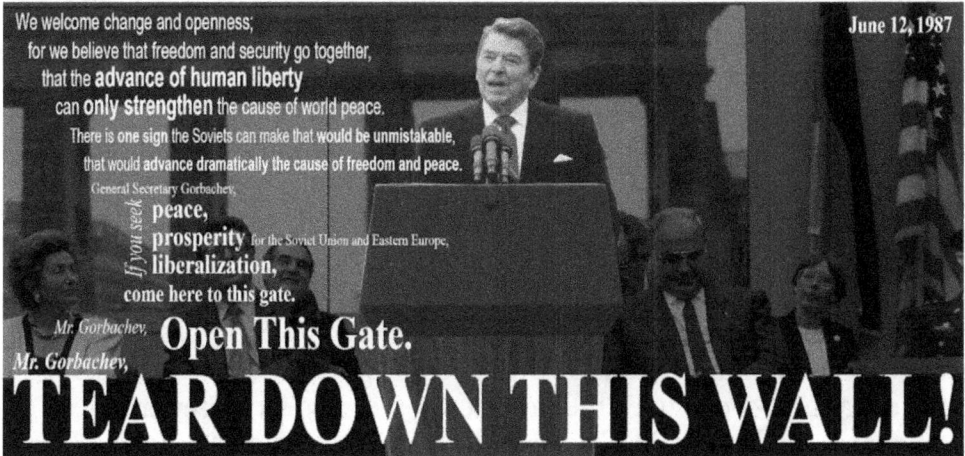

We welcome change and openness;
for we believe that freedom and security go together,
that the **advance of human liberty**
can **only strengthen** the cause of world peace.
There is one sign the Soviets can make that would be unmistakable,
that would advance dramatically the cause of freedom and peace.
General Secretary Gorbachev,
If you seek **peace,**
prosperity for the Soviet Union and Eastern Europe,
liberalization,
come here to this gate.
Mr. Gorbachev, **Open This Gate.**
Mr. Gorbachev,
TEAR DOWN THIS WALL!

June 12, 1987

Mr. Gorbachev, tear down this wall!

Would this work in California? On April 10, 2019, I listened intently to the Rush Limbaugh program as I often do. A caller hit the nail on the head with a simple suggestion but at first it seemed like it was a silly idea. It had to sink in to be recognized for its brilliance.

In the spirit of the Reagan speech, the caller suggested letting the whiners in California now led by Gavin Newsom have their way. Tear down the border wall separating the small strip at the bottom of California from Mexico. Newsom is against California helping the US protect its borders and has suggested he is even prepared to take the National Guard off California's border.

Newsom has issues with Trump on the border wall and he called Trump out recently when he said: "A 2,000-mile wall is a monument to stupidity, not just vanity, to stupidity," It's pure political theater. He creates these sideshows, this political theatre, this political grandstanding."

In referring to the president's attempts to spend billions of dollars on building the border wall, Newsom said it's a distraction to steer away from more substantive solutions to the immigration problem.

Newsom went on to defend a $25 million proposed California program to assist asylum seekers who cross the border into the state because he affirms the federal government isn't doing its job.

The governor vowed 'sanctuary to all who seek it' In his inauguration speech but he does not like the Idea of Trump sending detained illegals to his Sanctuary State.

"The federal government turns its back to them, turns a blind eye to them. California will not. They won't do their job, we'll do their job," he said. Yet, he does not want them to live in his state. The governor still insists he wants to work with the president on emergency preparedness and emergency planning. We'll see. So far, Newsom won't take any from the caravans.

The caller on the Rush Limbaugh show heard this Newsom disrespect just like I did and you did and he wants California to be on its own and on their knees rather than have them a cocky part of the union that spews such nasty crap about our President.

I admit that I never heard Newsom or anybody else suggest that Trump should take down the wall at San Diego or any other California border wall just because California is not pro-wall. But, why not?

The more I thought about it, the more I thought, why not? Let the illegal community overrun Southern California and then relieve them of their pain after they get on their knees and ask for help at the border and give the President some help in solving the problem for America.

Rush at first, like me was not sure, but now, as we will see in the radio broadcast exchange that I captured from the show archives, he has had a rethinking. The gentleman's idea of ripping the wall down like Trump as Reagan calling to Gorbachev to **bring down the wall**. (if you don't want it) is actually a pretty good idea. If California does not want the rest of the country's help, let them figure out how to solve their own issues.

Let's go through this radio broadcast as it occurred less than two weeks ago right now as I write this sentence:

Do Democrats want the California wall?
Apr 10, 2019

RUSH: This is Rick. Rick is in Munster, Indiana, and it's great to have you with us today, sir. Hello.

CALLER: Hi, Rush. Great to talk to you. Hey, great to get through to talk to you also.

RUSH: Big deal, I know. Congrats.

CALLER: Concerning the border wall with Mexico and paraphrasing Ronald Reagan, "Mr. President, tear down this wall," but only in California. President Trump, I think, should agree with Nancy Pelosi that in the state of California, the wall along the Mexican border is immoral, like she said. He should declare California an outlaw sanctuary state, and order that the wall be taken down, starting at the Pacific Ocean and working eastward toward Arizona. The state of —

RUSH: (laughing) You want these people to eat their words —

Me: I know I want them to eat their words as they prevent us all from being safe.

CALLER: That's right.

RUSH: — and you want them to be eaten by what would happen as a result?

CALLER: That's right. The state of California would have to contend with this flood of illegals crossing the border, and the federal government will not provide the state any assistance. No apprehensions. No detentions. But the federal government… All federal property like naval bases — Camp Pendleton, National Parks and stuff — will be vigorously defended. At that point, Nancy Pelosi will have to concede that a wall works or suffer the consequences of her moral righteousness.

RUSH: (sigh) Well, you know —

CALLER: It's not gonna happen, but it would be fun to hear Trump threaten such an action.

RUSH: Ah, it's an interesting talking point, though. It's a great exercise, teachable moment. You do have these Democrats out there like Pelosi talking about how walls are immoral and they don't work. California has a wall. If they didn't? They're overrun without a wall. California is gone to the Republicans politically and has been for a while because of this, but it's an interesting thing to tell people.

You know it will never happen, but warn people. Most people don't even know there is a wall in California — I mean, other than people near it. You tell 'em, "Tear down the wall that's separating Mexico from California," and you watch what happens. "N-n-no, don't do that! Don't!" "Why? Why are you afraid of that?" "The state would be overrun."

"But that's what you want. You've got sanctuary cities. You've got welfare systems set up. You have education, health care for illegals. What's a few more?" It's an excellent way of illustrating things — and if it did happen, you would have some people clamoring for it to stop, like Pelosi and Feinstein and all the others out there who are standing in the way of doing this around the country. I'm glad you called, Rick. Thanks much.

Thank Your Rick and Rush for a great perspective. Back when I was a kid I can recall Barry Goldwater's big ad comment:

In your heart, you know he is right!

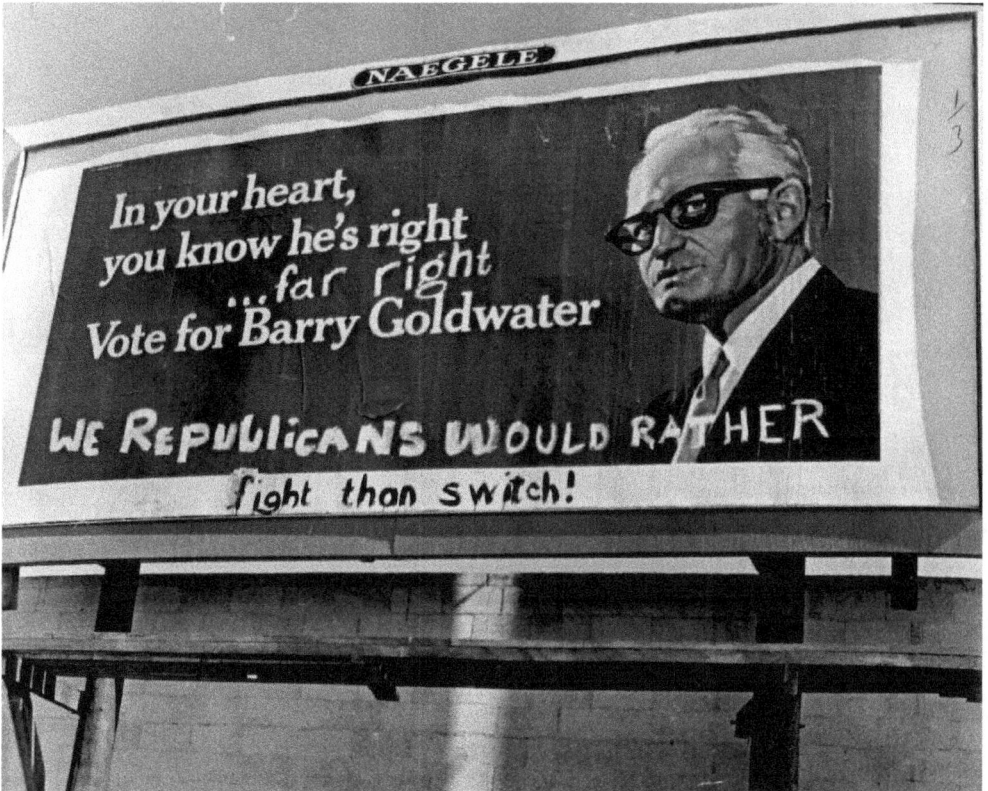

When JFK, my guy, was assassinated in 1963, Lyndon Johnson became president and ran again against Barry Goldwater, who was the master of conservatism. My dad and I, (I was a teenager) liked Kennedy and then Johnson seemed OKt after that. Neither of us were clear thinking then. Actually, Goldwater would have been a better president than Johnson but those days cannot be relived. Sometimes people choose a party rather than the better man.

I have little respect for politicians today. When I ran for the Congress in 2010, I took on every challenger who called me a politician as I see it as a dirty word. My favorite political movie is *Meet John Doe*. If you want a big clue as to how I feel about politics, see this movie. It ought to be required viewing for anybody seeking office. And there should be a test!

Talk to the Hand

Would anybody listen if I screamed out that I wanted California's wall to be torn down because they won't defend the wall at all? Maybe! But highly unlikely!

Why would the Congress of the US listen to me or you or any of the John Does out there? Most individuals feel that their needs and opinions are not taken very seriously by elected representatives who occupy the hallowed chambers of our government structures. We would call it a communication break-down but there really is no communication.

Despite our inability to get legislators to know our side of important issues, such as taxation, jobs, illegal aliens, etc., and more recently, bailouts, and healthcare, and sending California to the wolves by tearing down their wall, we treat them with too much respect. We intrinsically know that they care only about the desires and opinions of pressure groups, lobbyists, corporate executives and owners, as well as the plain old rich. Don't we know that?

Only these voices reach our representatives. Yet, time and time again, we the people affected let them off the hook. Politicians cut themselves off from their electorate by choice to be spared from accountability. Yet, whenever necessary, they make a resurfacing experience and always in time for the next election. Why are we so nice to them? We surely should not be so nice. We should take more appropriate action.

You may not see them in action when they work the halls of congress but you do see them work the wedding halls when it is the height of the election season. In Congress, the typical representative appears to have some sort of godly mandate, on the basis of which, whatever they put forward must be good for everybody.

However, whether it is a good idea or not, and they rarely are, you know the idea more than likely came from the whispers of the graft-giving chosen elite. Politicians do not serve most of their electorate and they get away with it because again, we do not hold them accountable, and we do not break their pattern by showing up on their doorsteps with our needs. We should!

It's time to fire them!

What would happen to the placid world of the politician if its constituency took them to task? What might happen to these politicos if the citizens suddenly became extremely active? How would the elected representative handle such a massive increase in constituent contact? Would they become beneficent, magnanimous or munificent? Or would they choose the hermitage approach and lock the gates and doors and hope the rabble will go away?

Especially if we think they would never put up with our entreaties, we should deluge them anyway and help power our representative democracy back to working order. In our hearts, we know we would see nothing more than congressional aides coming out of the woodwork to "see if they can help matters." That of course is code for "see if they can shut us up!" And, for their lack of effort on our behalf, we should do the only humane thing to our representatives: fire them! Throw the bums out. They've had their day.

Regular guys are taking notice

There is a clear and fundamental problem with our government, even when we are on different sides of most of the other issues. In Mitt Romney' s campaign, he said that Washington was "broken." With Obama in his day, it may have been just "broke." Thanks for the cash , China.

Either way, before Trump the easy forgetting cannot recall that it was almost beyond repair. For the broken government that gave us the infamous Bush Dubai Ports deal, whose ex-Presidents represent foreign nations, and who have passed laws such as the "uniform labeling of products" fiasco, a fellow citizen of mine, Rik Reppe, a regular guy and self described performer, writer, raconteur, and occasional business geek, ripped the establishment a new item in his blog at the URL below. Good Americans hate bad politicians.

http://reppe.blogs.com/reppecom/2006/03/because_we_get_.html

Reppe believes that we the people get exactly what we deserve because we elect these talking heads and empty suits, who owe their allegiance to some corporation someplace. To demonstrate the rage that is out there in cyberspace about what an absolutely abysmal bunch of political louts run our government, I picked two paragraphs from Rik's rants on the labeling topic. Though many things at the time were truly Obama's fault, even more as days goes by, lack of representation is not a recent phenomenon. These caught Rik's ire, for example, a while back in March, 2006

"But why should we believe the House of Representatives is
looking out for us and not sucking at the corporate t...t? That's
easy. You know the House has got your back...you know they're
grandstanding for votes...on any and all issues on which no public
hearings are held. Because we all know that politicians who are
looking out for the people hate it when those efforts are brought to
the attention of the people. Hate it, hate it, hate it. The last
thing...the very last thing in the whole wide political universe any
politician wants to do in an election year is to trumpet efforts to
help the voters thus securing easy camera and soundbite time.
...
And ain't it grand that on the same day the Senate passed a
completely impotent and toothless "lobbying reform" bill that
contains no actual provision to enforce the increased disclosure
the impotent and toothless product of their collective minds
created (passed by a vote of 90-8 proving that as much as I want
this to be a Republican issue it f...ing well isn't) it takes up an issue
that had been voted down by every Congress since 1994 and is
only back to the influence of lobbyists? You may hate what our
Senators are doing but you gotta love that kind of brazen chutzpa,
don't you?"

They work for someone else

The chasm between electors and the elected is widening as we speak. The
John Does and the Jane Q. Publics have lost faith in their representatives.
Many have become fully disinterested in the political process, though the
healthcare "debate" and the fresh air at the "Town Meetings" may be just
the cure for this malaise.

For some time, with good reason, the public has felt disenfranchised from
the basic right of a citizen to participate in the democracy. Some may
handle this by ignoring politics. Others may find alternative ways to
attempt to influence the course of events, sometimes through friends and
associates, but not always with very positive results.

Sometimes as we have seen in our history, the frustration of humans in
our democracy leads to violence as in the civil rights movements and the
anti-war rallies of the 1960's and the riots in Los Angeles in the

1990's. Are we there again? Perhaps the main reason that the system even seems to work is that constituents do not make many demands -- at least till now, and like Reppe says,

"We Get The Government We Deserve."

Why not just remove the California wall and see what happens to those that do not want the wall? Then, of course when they beg, let's fix it.

Do we deserve any fine government when we do not hold the rapscallions accountable? This is the root cause that permits politicians, masquerading as our representatives, to represent other interests. It is an understatement to suggest that representatives are out of touch with the will of the people. Even the newly elected begin to share the wealth of their constituency with others as they begin their "service." They have this need to redistribute income and now they are redistributing healthcare.

This is a common malady of the often elected and the newly elected are quickly infected. For a politician, it's "catchier" than the Swine Flu. Elected "representatives" have no problem taking your money and buying votes with it -- even if there is nothing left in the treasury.

Until they got caught by John Q., how many of the "honorables" voted originally to have the non-working and the illegal aliens receive the tax rebate of 2008? This trick was like buying future votes but the motivation was the same. It wasn't really intended for the downtrodden, hapless, illegal foreign national struggling to make ends meet. Not a chance. It was to puff up the elected to demonstrate their magnanimity and vote-worthiness.

Besides your money, they will also take your means of earning a living if it serves their purposes. To please their corporate sponsors, they have no problem taking your job and giving it to a foreign national, either here in the U.S. or in the worker's home country, in China or India. They have just one mission and it is accomplished if they get elected again. The next term of office, not the current one, is all that matters. We get the government we deserve.

Tear down this wall, Gov. Newsom

So, here we are in this book in this chapter wondering if we willed it, would President Trump rip down the wall in the skinny stretch of land at the bottom of California that separates San Diego and other areas from the Baja in Mexico, including Tijuana. I like the idea more and more—the more I think about it.

Here we are moving along and the next thing I would like to talk about. A good man in the 2005 time period wrote some great essays which I would like to share with you now. They are on the topic of illegal immigration and California. They are intended to get your blood boiling. Enjoy the next four chapters from Thomas Dawson.

Chapter 7 Illegal Aliens and Immigration

Essays by Thomas Dawson

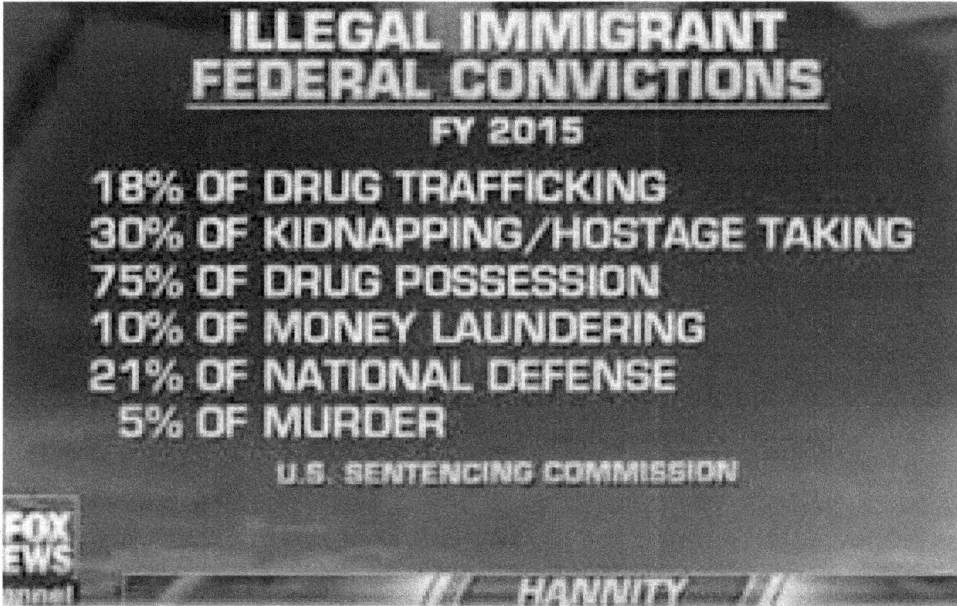

ILLEGAL IMMIGRANT FEDERAL CONVICTIONS
FY 2015
18% OF DRUG TRAFFICKING
30% OF KIDNAPPING/HOSTAGE TAKING
75% OF DRUG POSSESSION
10% OF MONEY LAUNDERING
21% OF NATIONAL DEFENSE
5% OF MURDER
U.S. SENTENCING COMMISSION
FOX NEWS
HANNITY

Illegal immigration is no longer a victimless crime.

In the next four chapters, including this one, we look at the insightful essays of Thomas Dawson as he originally wrote them in 2005 with some minor modifications to bring them up-to-date. Please enjoy them as Tom would love it that you read his thoughts. It is easy to agree with Thomas Dawson.

Is It is amazing in this small world that there are people who think like we do. About ten years ago, as I wrote my first books about the topic of illegal aliens and the lax border enforcement we employ in California and the rest of the border states, I found a gentleman named Thomas Dawson who knew the problem well. We talked electronically a few times.

I told him how much I loved what he had written about this American problem and he wished me well and told me to include whatever I felt would help the situation in the book in process at the time. It was titled: *Taxation Without Representation.*

Thomas Dawson is among the missing today. I wish I could locate him so we could talk again and so that I could send him some of his work in book form. Mr. Dawson did give me permission to repeat his writings and I have done so here and in a several few other places. I hope you enjoy the work of this great writer as I do. It all began with a surprise in my email after contacting Mr. Dawson.

Surprise in Email

While I was researching the first edition of my book titled *Taxation Without Representation*, I came across numerous anecdotes, many of which were nothing short of amazing and phenomenally insightful. One thing I have learned in my 71 years (my 72nd Birthday is next) is that nobody knows it all and as a corollary, there is something brilliant that is ready to be discovered every day.

I was so impressed with the writings of Thomas Dawson, both in content and style that I wrote him a few months before the first edition of my first patriotic book was completed. I asked if I could use his material in the referenced book. At the time, I had intended to use some excerpts of his works in the main body of some of the chapters in which his insights applied. But, when I received Tom's note right before I submitted the first edition, I had to make other arrangements.

I thought about an insertion here or there and then I decided that, since Mr. Dawson offered no strings on his granting permission for his works, I would print them as full essays rather than excerpts. It is all for your reading pleasure and I give him the full credit he deserves. This was his note to me. I have never met him but you can feel the goodness of this gentleman in his words:

Mr. Kelly:

Sorry I couldn't get back to you sooner. You are more than welcome to use any of my material at your discretion, either in agreement with my thinking or in disagreement. You need not give credit. This old bumpkin will be delighted if you can encourage someone to think about the world in which the next generation will live. Provoke thought whenever possible.

I wish you personal satisfaction in your endeavors, and please inform me when your book is available.

With warm regards

Tom

How can you beat that? So I took the poetic license given to me by Thomas Dawson to provide four of his essays from 2005. They had been published online in the American Chronicle. Please enjoy these and encourage others to think about the world in which the next generation will live. "Provoke thought whenever possible."

Difficulties Lie Ahead

These are good pieces for you to have in your personal library and there is good news. There are a number of other works by Thomas Dawson on the Internet available for your reading.

About *Taxation Without Representation*

Obviously I wrote this book to point out the travesty and the reality of taxation without representation in the modern age. Topics from taxes to the fact that hizzoners, all over the U.S. at all levels of government, who are not representing the American people, make up the bulk of this book. The culprit in most cases is the corporation but with major complicity of our "honorables." If I were Thomas Dawson, I would have said that the purpose of this book is to "encourage someone to think about the world in which the next generation will live. Provoke thought whenever possible."

The good news is that I am finished with what I was going to do and if you had been reading this in the first edition, as the essays were in the Appendix, you would have been almost finished with this book. You have the four essays by Thomas Dawson now to read beginning with this chapter in *Hasta La Vista California*. I predict these will be a treat for you to read.

However, the issues in the essays as the issues raised in thismy Taxation book are no more solved because you will have completed this task in these few pages, than if you do not. These are big problems to solve. Mr. Dawson points these out in his essays. We have a lot of work to do in helping our brothers and sisters in America take back control of our government. It won't be easy. But, with the risk of Barack Obama, Nancy Pelosi, and Harry Reid in charge for eternity, we must take action. Thankfully, two of these names are gone from the political scene and now a great man, IMHO sent from God to help America, Donald Trump, is out president, and a fine president I might add.

I will sign off my part of this chapter and the next three right now, leaving you in the capable hands of Mr. Thomas Dawson. Know that the difficulties ahead for our country regarding illegal immigration are solvable if we watchfully pay attention to our government and call it to task on what it must do. I feel confident leaving you to these four essays and then to yourself and all the other selves like you and I, and Thomas Dawson.

God Bless You -- and our America.

Here is the first of four essays by Mr. Dawson.

Essays of Thomas Dawson:
Illegal Aliens and Immigration

By Thomas Dawson
June 03, 2005

Essay 1 of 4

We do not have an immigration problem with Mexico. We do have a border problem with Mexico. Without making more jokes about Homeland Security, borders are important. Without borders, there is no country…or security. Some public political debate has begun, but don't expect too much.

The easiest way to win a political argument in today's world, particularly if your position is without practical merit is to confuse the issues. The proponents of open borders, and there are many, use this method to make their arguments. They never use the correct term "illegal alien". They refuse to view these people as either illegal or aliens. The most that one can hope for, is that they will use the term "undocumented immigrants".

You can bet that after one or two minutes of discussion the term will degenerate into just "immigrants". Without any qualifier, most of what they say is correct. Most importantly, whatever you say in their context sounds racist. Of course, we live in an age of labels and buzzwords. If you allow such people to get away with it, they will play the game of "gotcha" as they try to stick a label on you. Unfortunately, this is not a child's game.

If the media polls are correct, the American people overwhelmingly recognize the gravity of the situation and would like to correct it. We're not talking about Democrats or Republicans here nor Conservatives or Liberals. When we take the labels off, you'll find that most American citizens can and often do, think!

Alas, there is little hope for any real change to take place in the near future. There is a great and growing disconnect between modern politicians and the people they are supposedly representing. So there will be a great deal of gamesmanship or slight of hand to convince people that they are looking into the situation. In reality, the politicians will continue to stall any useful action for the sake of their "financial constituency."

Some discussion at the federal level has finally begun again, and a few really big political names are making a lot of noise. But in a typical stalling tactic, the discussion is not about closing the borders. The talk is about those illegal aliens that are already here and many more that will come, as we make plans for them. Their only concern is what will be the final criteria to make them underclass citizens? Discussions with this kind of detailed minutia can be dragged out for a very long time… and they will be. Meanwhile, first Vicente Fox and now, Andrés Manuel López Obrador are sending us as many of his people as they can; as fast as they can.

The federal politicians are beholden to organized interest groups for financial support and really find it difficult, if not impossible to stand up for their people 'back home' on any major issue where a lot of corporate money is at stake.

Amnesty for Mexican illegal aliens was granted a few years ago (Reagan, 1986), and since then the border control has been relaxed. Now we are being told that there is no alternative for a humane solution without again providing amnesty. Don't listen to the politicians; they have no intention of closing the Mexican borders until, and only if forced to do so. It is only a ploy to bring in more cheap labor for exploitation.

The failed corporate religion of Globalization in the name of 'free trade' is really a search for the cheapest labor available. Corporations have greased the wheels of government and momentum is steamrolling any public opposition.

Manufacturers are now allowed to 'globalize' by outsourcing their labor costs to the cheapest of overseas labor, and retailers can 'globalize' by purchasing the cheapest products they can find manufactured overseas, and thus they can both increase their profits. They can also claim increases in productivity in a single stroke as they reduce their costs. The question arises. Why should agriculture and service industries that cannot move overseas not share in Globalization? The simple answer is they can. Simply have the politicians "move the mountain to Mohammed".

Now that the government allows corporations to bring in really cheap "illegals" for the service and agriculture industries, they too are receiving the labor/cost benefits of 'Globalization'. Not to mention the hundreds of thousands of "guest workers" that have already been imported to work as engineers, IT technicians, etc which are hired at only 50% to 80% of the going rate in this country, thus holding down the wage scales of the middle class and increasing corporate profits. With a single stroke of the pen and government grease, anything can be made legal. Seems like a sensible way to reduce wages and push profits up.

To paraphrase Milton Friedman, "Corporate executives, provided they stay within the law, have no responsibilities in their business activities other than to make as much money for their stockholders as possible." Milton Freeman is absolutely right. A corporation has no responsibility to anyone. It is not a person. It is a legal animal (entity) created by the law of a country. It is an animal without social conscience or concern for anything except profits.

If a corporation has any responsibility, it is only to the law of the country in which it operates. It is the duty of the country of origin to regulate and control its offspring. When a domestic corporation behaves badly, it should be disciplined. When a foreign company behaves badly, it should be disciplined and if it continues, refrained from doing business. Every country should set the rules for its own house.

If we allow "globalization" to wring out our middle class, we can easily lose the increased standard of living gained during the first quarter century after World War II. (Since then. our standard of living has gone nowhere. It has probably even declined a bit in the last quarter century.) Our problem is not with the natural ambitions of corporations. Our problem is with the deliberately calibrated reluctance of (the peoples?) representation in government to regulate with any care for or concern toward the public good.

In the long run though, the politicians at the state and local levels will have to face the reality of the economic situation. Continuing to assume low cost, near poverty level labor has a depressing effect on all wages over extended periods of time. Increases in poverty create demand for state and local services as well as lowering per capita taxes. Hospitals across the south to California have had to go into bankruptcy and some have closed because of expenses incurred by illegal aliens who are unable to pay. Many immigrants and illegal aliens have earnings low enough to qualify for welfare assistance.

At the same time, these states and local governments are experiencing lower per capita tax revenues as wages begin to drift downwards. The greatest increase in costs due to these illegal aliens and low-cost immigrants is, of course education.

Law enforcement and incarceration costs are also rising. It is estimated that in 2003, California alone, even after accounting for tax contributions from illegal aliens, the direct cost was more than $8,000,000,000 and total costs probably well in excess of $11,000,000,000. In 2019, the cost is approaching $30 billion and growing quickly. California can't even fix its roads, and this is just the beginning! All this is just part of the cost of subsidizing labor for the service industries.

As we erode the middle class and the consumer market begins to falter, the tax base will continue to shrink and tax revenues fall. After all, middle class working people pay the vast bulk of the tax burden. What will your town look like as state and local governments slash services by 15, 20, or even 25%?

Increasing numbers of illegal aliens and poverty level immigrants cause economic and social disruption. On the other hand, carefully managed legal immigration will contribute to the economic and social growth of the country. Bringing in large numbers of qualified people to fill jobs (at current rates of pay) where there are labor or professional shortages means more contributing citizens. Encouraging carefully managed increases in immigration is important to this country, both as an economic contribution and by increasing the population underpinning.

Do we have problems in agriculture? Certainly! How many people do we need to help us out? The government says that we already have between eight and a half million and eleven million illegal aliens. Others estimate between eighteen and twenty million. The likely probability is that we have between twelve and fifteen million. This means that the illegal aliens represent about four percent or slightly more of our population.

Author Brian W. Kelly says there are 60 million illegal interlopers in the country right now. See his book on the subject: *60 Million Illegal Aliens in America!!!: A simple, America-first solution.* https://www.amazon.com/dp/1947402137

This is way more than one out of every twenty-five people. Should we bring in more people for every crop and then let them melt into the general population and continue to grow a permanent underclass of cheap labor, undermining the wage base of the entire country? Of course not! There must be a constant, but controlled rotation of workers for agriculture. Perhaps permanent labor arrangements could be had with foreign labor at a slightly better rate of pay. Assuming we want to continue to subsidize agriculture with cheap labor, there are a number of possibilities.

Alternatively, we may want to consider taking the gratuitous profits away from corporate owners of our subsidized, socialized agricultural enterprises. Or perhaps even doing away with socialized agriculture and even corporate welfare entirely! I am sure that politicians would find this to be a national security issue far greater than merely open borders! But that is a subject for another day.

Even if we continue to subsidize agriculture with (dare I say dirt cheap) labor, this does not mean that every business should be entitled to hire at poverty wage levels. Inviting immigration at or near poverty level wages is not good for this country's public good. Let the service businesses pay a little more and charge a little more. We can pay more for the services or pay a lot more for the subsidies.

Workers in the construction trades have been a part of the middle class for the last fifty years. Now, (2005) with the strongest continuous housing boom and the highest prices for houses in our history, construction workers are experiencing falling wages and unemployment due to unemployed cheap and often illegal labor. It's past time to consider where we are heading.

It's also time to close our borders and then begin a serious discussion. In any case, any political talk about solving the immigration problem without first closing the borders is pure deception, and a sham!

This Thomas Dawson essay was written in 2005. What if we had built the wall back then. Think about how far ahead we would be today.

Chapter 8 All Immigration Problems Solved

Essay 2 of 4

By Thomas Dawson
June 11, 2005

A panel set up by the Council on Foreign Relations wants Americans to stop thinking of themselves as United States citizens and to think of themselves as just North Americans. The panel has published a report called "Building a North American Community" in which it proposes a single common border around the three countries. The purpose is to create a free flow of goods and labor between the countries. They hope to accomplish this over the next five years, by 2010.

Note: There has not been much if any progress on this initiative over the last fourteen years. Thank God for small favors.

It seems unfortunate that Asia is not adjacent to us so that they could provide even larger numbers of even cheaper labor for the corporate citizens of this new world order, that has now completely bought out our government.

In reality, this is just another salvo in the battle to create an aura of inevitability around the idea of globalization. The destruction of borders for the purpose of moving cheap labor is only one facet of this new deity. If we can be convinced that we are caught up in the inevitable tide of history, then the right to choose has been taken from us.

It has become the obligation of our highly paid government officials to prepare the middle-class citizens for changes that their employers intend to make in this world. Certainly, if they can pull it off, this would be a great step forward toward globalization. In any case, these kinds of discussions create another great stall to keep the borders open.

Globalization, the idea of a 'One World Government" is not new. We fought WWII so that the world would not become fascist. We endured the cold war so that the world would not become communist. Since then we have worried that the UN would take over the world and form a world government. Now we find that the seeds of our cultural destruction are to be found in the very basis of our democratic free enterprise system.

This country has always indulged the corporate community as one of our children, giving it status, favoring it over any other public interest. We have asked little in return. We mistakenly assumed that in return for this favored status, these entities would naturally provide employment for our citizens with wages sufficient to sustain an improving standard of living in the long run.

For the past thirty years we have considered failure in this regard as only a temporary setback. Now we find that sustaining a reasonable standard of living or even the continued employment of middle-class citizens is not on the agenda, not even a consideration of the corporate community.

Unfortunately, this unwritten contract or understanding does not exist in principle any more than it does in writing. What did we expect? We have failed to discipline this child of ours and now it has become a self-serving tyrant. You probably thought the "Robber Barons" were tough. I can assure you that, as Ronald Reagan would say "You ain't seen nothing yet!"

We are spectators to the birthing of this new world order called Globalization. Large international corporations, which even now are no longer responsible to, nor contributing to any public good, have high hopes of running the world as a single cooperative trading entity. The very concept of traditional nation-states will become irrelevant. Large trading companies will run this brave new world on an "as needed" basis.

Nation-states will become reduced to mere cultural centers. These will become the transport systems of the trading companies, with which they will trade in people and goods wherever required. A managers' dream! Indeed, the managers are already, at this very moment, the aristocrats of our time. Globalization is to become the manifestation of their consolidation of power.

Managers have already replaced the capitalists and entrepreneurs in the world of international corporations. Only minor players and small companies are still willing or need to risk their money in today's environment. International companies do not invest in new enterprises or attempt to compete with other companies.

They either buy out small companies that appear to be successful within a given market, or merge with their competitors. In either case, market share is increased and a secure established market is acquired without risk. Little is left to chance; they are managing everything; most especially the governments of the western world. Management has finally trumped leadership in business, as well as in government.

To be sure, at the moment they still need other companies with whom they can appear to compete. This is not an overt conspiracy. It is rather, a "gentleman's agreement"; an understanding, if you will. For the moment, at least, the illusion of competition must be maintained. But, consider that just this week, (circa 2005) Toyota is taking the poison pill because they fear someone will take them over due to their recent financial success. In the dawn of this global environment, the realization of any entrepreneurial success will probably become sufficient reason for your immediate demise, as expanding international interests will try to gobble you up.

Our enormous financial institutions will even provide money for little fish to eat big fish, providing the big fish have control over secure markets. Because of the low risk factor in these kinds of takeovers, these financial institutions only require a relative premium over the current interest rate.

The United States has been an easy mark for the globalization movement due to the close ties developed by corporations between themselves and financially dependent and greedy government officials, readily managed by corporate money. These corporations are, to our elected representatives, their "financial constituents". The pharmaceutical industry alone has two people lobbying on every congressman.

Asian countries may not be so easy; they only needed corporate connections with the west until they were locked into the relatively affluent western economies. They have the world's largest cheap labor force and are now graduating great numbers of highly educated people. They will soon have the largest and cheapest well-educated work force in the world. Their economies have gained momentum and as they grow, they become somewhat insulated and independent of western style corporate persuasion.

They will appear to tolerate a certain amount of corporate "rule making" such as "intellectual property" only so long as it serves their interests. They understand the greed of our corporations and are happily building "feed lots" for them. When all is said and done, Asia will not view these international corporations as their own children, to be coddled and upon whom they will stake their future. When these corporations have been fattened and can no longer contribute to the national interest, their assets will be nationalized; gobbled up by some "really big fish" that are hardly manageable.

Chapter 9 Labor Arbitrage? Better Known as Cheap Labor

Essay 3 of 4

By Thomas Dawson
October 12, 2005

"When you can't relocate the plant to Mexico for various reasons, you can still produce cheaply in the US by hiring illegal labor from Mexico"

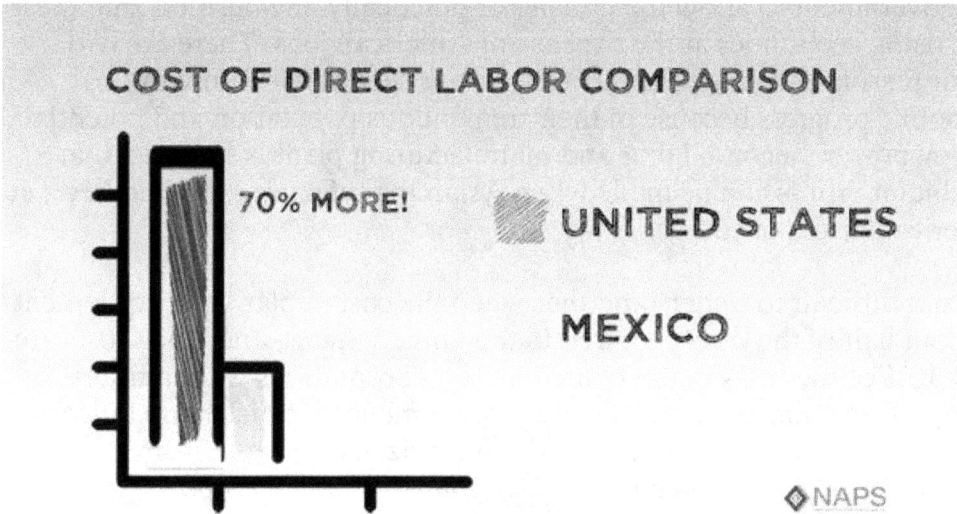

COST OF DIRECT LABOR COMPARISON

70% MORE!

UNITED STATES

MEXICO

◆NAPS

It's time we stopped kidding ourselves! The continuation of the illegal immigration from Mexico is the direct intention of our government. When a government enforces a law, we are inclined to think that the enforcement is their duty. However, when a government does not enforce the law, we are inclined to think that perhaps it is their choice. It is not. Not when it concerns the security of our borders. Of course, there are reasons for our government's overt support for the illegal immigration on the southern border.

Since the end of the 'Cold War', our international companies have turned their attention and swayed the attention of our government toward the domination of world economics without concern for the domestic consequences. This variation on the economic system is referred to as the neo-liberal economic system and is generally understood as globalization. It is part and parcel of the modern democratic theory as expounded by the United States and is to be imposed upon the rest of the world, by force if necessary. Even our children understand by now that globalization favors corporate profits above the common good, or anything else.

The most obvious example of the effects of globalization in this country is our relationship with Asia. Over the past few years, we have not only outsourced our jobs, but have moved our manufacturing to the Asian countries, especially China and India. Corporate money has influenced our government to allow the transfer of practically any business into these new rising economies at the expense of American jobs. There are two major reasons for this interest. First, Asia is seen as the future of economic progress because of their tremendous population and potential buying power. Second, labor and manufacturing plant is so cheap that exorbitant profits can be made when Asian manufactures are sold here; at American prices of course.

It is not difficult to understand that when the cost of plant and equipment is about half of the costs required in the United States, and labor costs are only 10% of the costs in the United States, corporations will naturally choose to manufacture in Asia. Our government officials are no longer concerned about the common good of its citizens; rather they are interested in their personal gain to be acquired through corporate influence.

At home, our service industries can only exist as long as there is enough money circulating among the middle and lower classes to support the consumerism. Our financial industry can only continue to exist as long as the asset bubble continues. Our only real source of income is our military weapons business. We supply most of the world's weapons. Where does the money come from to maintain our economy? It is the consistent growth of our national and personal debts that maintains the momentum of our economy. Our government needs to maintain that momentum for a while longer.

As far as our corporations are concerned, the writing is on the wall. Real, or long-term investment will be made in Asia where a huge population with rising incomes will eventually dominate the economic world. The unemployed population in China alone is greater than the entire population of the United States. As the income of the average American citizen continues to erode, we are viewed by the corporate world as a mature market.

For years, the United States has not been a prime market for investment. Only in the past two years has the Trump Administration begun to turn this all around as companies, benefitting from less regulation and lower taxes are investing in America again.

For a time, the mantra was to reap the profits of past investments and maintain the cash cow as long as possible, or at least until a prosperous Asian economy can be built. Unfortunately, until Trump, it was obvious that our government supported this corporate view, regardless of what their lips told us.

At the turn of the century, these investments would not have happened. There were laws against unfair trade, concerning environmental issues, unfair labor practices, and a plethora of other rules and considerations for the public good. From 2005, many of these laws have been expunged or relaxed in the name of deregulation to allow for the international exploitation of labor. This is our government at work in behalf of their corporate constituencies.

Lest they lose their corporate sponsors, our media for years has been blaming Asia and especially China for the loss of our jobs and their excessive use of 'our' oil. It is our own government that encourages companies to invest in foreign countries, even to the point of awarding tax breaks for doing so. It is our own government that for years encouraged the displacement of American workers with cheaper foreign workers. China is not the villain here. It is our own government encouraging and aiding international corporations to move their business overseas in search of that Holy Grail, profits.

What about corporations that are not international in nature? Our government is doing its best to take care of them as well. It has deliberately brought in well over twenty million illegal Mexicans to work at menial wages and continues to dilute the work force. Of course, the government will explain that farm labor is still in short supply and we need more workers there. It seems that 'illegals' don't want to farm either.

They are coming in faster than the great immigration of the late nineteenth and early twentieth century. To be sure many of them eventually earn more than minimum wages. However, they can secure few, if any rights and are treated poorly. They do not generally get health benefits, nor do they get retirement benefits. Just as the international companies can exploit cheap labor, a similar arrangement has been made for the national companies. Labor is arbitraged just as any other commodity.

Our population is estimated at somewhat less than three hundred million people (2005). If we have only twenty million illegal immigrants, it means that one out of every fifteen people in this country is illegal. It is a significantly higher portion in the work force. Author Brian W. Kelly writes about there being 60 million illegals in America.

Notice that even in the rebuilding of New Orleans, the prevailing labor rates were not be paid to workers. The contracts were generally given out without competitive bidding at cost plus, to insure corporate profits to preferred companies. Restricting labor expenses was the only means to hold down costs. For some strange reason there is a faux shortage of workers. The government is bringing people willing to work from Central America. Is this because construction is just one more type of work that Americans won't do? Many of them will probably remain in this country to further dilute the work force. Meanwhile the poor of New Orleans have been dispersed around the country and will probably not be heard from again.

Reducing labor costs is the mantra of our time. This first attempt to dismantle Social Security is only the beginning. Many of our corporations are hiring illegal immigrants and do not pay any benefits. Other corporations will soon be crying that they cannot compete if they have to pay for health benefits or pension plans or perhaps even paid holidays. Our government intends to get cheap labor for their corporations by leveling the labor of the world at the expense of the American citizen. We have embraced a Darwinian system of economics to the detriment of our citizens! Or is this the Intelligent Design at work? In either case, it looks like plain old government sponsored greed.

Unrestricted illegal immigration is not a solution.

Replacing American workers with illegal foreign nationals is not a solution.

For California, an acceptable solution would be to tear down the M/C wall and permit all the illegals to find sanctuary in the biggest sanctuary state in the nation. Permit secession but do not permit the new foreign nationals to cross the new border into Nevada or Arizona

Chapter 10 Coin of the Realm

Essay 4 of 4

By Thomas Dawson
November 14, 2005

Since World War II our political entanglements with the rest of the world have been increasingly, rightly or wrongly, intended to secure or engender the business interests of our corporations. Suddenly our international companies are enamored with the opportunities to move labor-intensive segments of their business to foreign lands. They now view the United States as only a temporary cash cow; a mature market to be used until faster growing markets can be developed elsewhere.

At the same time, the interests of these corporations, who indirectly control our domestic economy, are often at odds with the welfare of our middle class. Corporate America has bought and paid for the influence of our politicians and since the end of the "cold war" they have been systematically reducing their liabilities and responsibilities with respect to the people that work for them in the quest for greater profits.

The primary and driving force of corporations is profit and this is as it should be. These corporations make up the engine of the American economy. However, the continued displacement of middle-class jobs, which are flowing out of the country at alarming rates, and the eroding standard of living, are the result of this same kind of thinking, and is encouraged by our present political structure. But, lest we forget, these United States were not intended as a land "of the corporation, by the corporation and for the corporation".

The national debt, trade deficits, middle-class wage erosion, immigration problems, health care costs, and a plethora of other national problems are all related to the political reality of "American style free trade" expanding throughout the world in the last forty years. We are told that these are normal, sequential economic changes taking place within our political system. Not so. The primary causation of most of these changes is the direct result of political pandering to corporate interests by our elected officials. Legislation should have some consideration of the "people" mentioned by our founding fathers.

The standard of living for the middle-class in this country has not improved in the last forty-years. In fact, consider that in the 1980's meatpackers in the Midwest, an industry dominated by black Americans, were making $19.00 per hour and because of the tough work, the wages were rising continually. But then, America got lax on the border and corporations tacitly began to solicit illegal foreign nationals for the work forces.

Meatpackers moved out of the metropolitan areas and built plants in the sticks and soon cheap housing followed and before long illegal foreign nationals dominated the work force and lived in squalor in new slums. Today, in 2019, the $19 wage from the 1980's is now about $8.00 per hour, barely above the minimum. Americans were duped by slimy politicians and did not know what hit them.

In fact, wages and the standard of living has declined for the vast majority of Americans—not just meatpackers. Real wages have fallen in some cases by more than 50%. Yet the GNP really is up! Because our (domestic?) companies are really making record profits! Our corporations are awash in money. At the same time the country is currently acquiring nearly THREE BILLION dollars of new debt through the trade deficit every day! Consider the National Debt. Disgraceful, and dangerous! A lot of other things are also going on here. This is a direct result of political pandering for corporate money. Politics is a very lucrative "profession". (Hardly anyone is doing this as a public service)

The truth is that politicians cannot survive without hoards of money. Ask anyone who has ever run for office how much it costs. Certainly the man on the street cannot support them. So where do they get it? Who has it? Only large corporations can make large contributions regularly over long periods of time. Most of it is given to the party's themselves so they can keep members in line through the use of the money spigot. It is tough to find an honest, independent politician today.

Not so long ago, this seemed like a reasonably good idea. Most of the large companies were entirely domestic and employed many people. The import/export companies were either bringing money into the country or buying products not available here. Many companies took on an international flavor while we were rebuilding Europe and Japan after WWII with their captive markets. Large amounts of money were acquired by American companies, along with a great deal of knowledge about other countries' economies and politics.

Great sums of money were spent on R&D and any new technology from around the world was developed quickly by the large US companies. All this employment was one of the major factors in building the American middle class. "What's good for General Motors is good for the Country" seemed to be a pretty accurate phrase if not an accurate quote. A direct connection between domestic GNP and the domestic standard of living was just assumed to be the natural condition. Unfortunately, in a few short years, this assumption would be ruptured.

In the middle 50's and 60's we began to see some interesting changes. We began to increase the imports of foreign goods, and some of our companies began to build plants in foreign countries and even exported products back home. Volkswagen began to sell cars over here. We could now buy an English Ford. This was good business for everyone. Business around the world was heating up. Everyone seemed to understand the rules and we all did well.

The Japanese suddenly burst on the scene. By the end of the 70's and into the 80's their quality cars were the best buy for the money. They had the best quality and Americans bought them. American car companies had manipulated the auto market for years for their own benefit and now the Japanese were encroaching on their very survival. Fortunately, Reagan was made to understand that we could not just watch such a large section of the middle-class workforce go down the drain. He effectively limited the number of Japanese imports.

When the Japanese asked to build automobiles over here and employ Americans, he invited them in. It was not the corporation he was protecting; it was the middle-class American workforce. (This ridiculous, Pro-American concern for the citizen did not go unnoticed by our growing international corporations and was soon to be changed.) The American manufacturers quickly improved the quality of their products and regained much of their reputation. Again, business was good for everybody.

Many corporations, especially those with international interests became extremely powerful as they did more business than many countries. It is only natural that they would want to extend their influence. For corporations this large, there is only one place of effective influence and that is the politician, domestic and foreign.

As large corporations are always looking for a profit advantage, they could hardly help noticing the disparity in wages between the developed countries and the under-developed ones. Japan has no natural resources and cannot compete with countries that do. They have to import, add value, and then export to make a profit. Business was so good that as their standard of living rose and they were over-employed, they "outsourced" the labor and for a few years had an enviable economy (read corporate profits). (Remember Japan bashing?)

Other international companies soon began to follow when the "cold war" came to a close. This kind of business was obviously not within the range of Reagan's pro-American thinking, but who cared? Corporations were making plenty of money and political contributions were rolling in! By the end of the 90's the world economy had so heated up that politicians easily convinced us that outsourcing cheap labor would not hurt the developed countries and that it would be of great benefit to the under-developed ones if only work rules, environmental considerations, and other regulations would be removed. (How benevolent they had become!) Besides, their corporate benefactors could make a lot of money.

We were having a domestic technology boom not unlike the automotive boom of the twenties. The slow-down (recession) of the early 90's seemed like a blip in an ever-growing world economic boom. To really make the corporations happy, the government got into the act with a bill to open so-called "free trade zones". And thus, NAFTA was born. This bill was sold as raising the Mexican standard of living and creating thousands of American jobs. A win, win bill! No one seriously believed American jobs would be created! In just a few short years this labor arbitrage reduced the average wage in Mexico to about half of what it was before NAFTA.

In the last twenty years, NAFTA began to hurt American workers and so, as promised in 2018, President Trump renegotiated the deal with Mexico and Canada. The new deal is called USMCA — the United States-Mexico-Canada Agreement. Trump actually cares about America's middle-class.

Our corporations for a while had been doing very well with NAFTA, because now they had something just as good or perhaps better than a free trade zone. They arranged another form of arbitrage, outsourcing their labor to Asian countries. Why pay 50 cents an hour to a Mexican when the Asians will work for 25 cents? The politicians even found ways to pay their corporate benefactors to outsource, by offering them tax breaks for doing it! No one can compete with Corporate America! Certainly, the American citizen can't!

Big farm Corporations have been trying to control congress since the 1930's. They have learned well and now other large corporations emulate them. All kinds of moneys are spent by the farm lobbies on strong incumbent congressmen and their families to "educate them" on the reasons for, and the importance of farm subsidies and other corporate interests. Along with his family and personal 'educational' benefits, the incumbent congressman will often get considerable moneys as contributions to his election campaign. Even larger contributions are made to his party (both parties for control purposes); of which his share will trickle down to him from a number of sources as long as he does not depart from the party interests (read corporate interests).

It's not hard to get a Congressman from Iowa to support a farm subsidy bill. It's a little harder to get a Delaware or Massachusetts Congressman to support it. One might think that this would take a bit of doing, as many times the congressman must support those things that are a direct detriment to his voting constituents. Most of the time however, his opponent will not even challenge him on these highly financed issues because his own funds from the party are controlled at a higher level. This system works so well that even pharmaceutical companies now spend rafts of money to "educate" doctors and their families at various resorts around the country. Currently, the pharmaceuticals are even "donating" to the FDA (for our benefit, of course). Understand that politicians can and do pass laws to benefit themselves, this is all perfectly legal…but…

At this point in time, the voter has been effectively disenfranchised. It is not that he does not have a choice; it is only that there is no choice. Whoever runs for office is beholden to the corporations for the money that is a necessary prerequisite to attain and retain the office. This, in effect, is the new democratic "one party" or "corporate party" system. The politician and his family live in a world filled with both perks and promise. If he cooperates and is in office for any considerable length of time, he is practically guaranteed a plum lifetime job consulting or lobbying for these same companies and thus greasing the wheels of other politicians. (Responsible companies always reward their good soldiers.)

The heavy hand of corporate influence on the members of congress is not a new problem. It has been a festering problem since the earliest days of our country. When the great majority of citizens were farmers, it didn't seem that lobbyists could do much harm. As corporate America grew and farming became more efficient, the trend was for more Americans to leave the farms and become employees of these new corporations.

In the last part of the nineteenth century, thinking people were becoming concerned that the interests of Corporate America and the country as a whole were not of a like nature. There was much concern that corporate money was controlling the outcome of most of the laws in this country, and something should be done to curb this influence. In his annual message to the congress in 1907, President Theodore Roosevelt stated "The need for collecting large campaign funds would vanish if Congress provided an appropriation for the proper and legitimate expenses of each of the great national parties, an appropriation ample enough to meet the necessity for thorough organization and machinery, which requires a great expenditure of money.

Then the stipulation should be made that no party receiving campaign funds from the Treasury should accept more than a fixed amount from any individual subscriber or donor, and the necessary publicity for receipts and expenditures could without difficulty be provided." This is an idea that is still mentioned from time to time.

Many, if not most of the legislation that is enacted helps one group of people at the expense of another. Such is the nature of laws. Laws against cartels and monopolies in favor of fairness to the other corporations and indeed the citizens are necessary and good for the health of our country, but only if the government chooses to enforce them. Laws passed against the middle-class Americans in favor of powerful corporations are not good for the health of our country. In theory, the elected officials are supposed to represent the voting public, not the corporate contributors. Passing legislation that will erode the middle class for the benefit of corporate profits is a crime against the citizenry.

You cannot blame a rat as a thief if you allow it to steal grain, nor blame a cat as a murderer if you allow it to kill rats. That is the very nature of these animals. You cannot blame corporations if you allow them to buy politicians. This is indeed the very nature of this animal. To paraphrase Milton Friedman, "Corporate executives, provided they stay within the law, have no responsibilities in their business activities other than to make as much money for their stockholders as possible." That is why we need laws and regulations, to determine exactly what is to be allowed.

You can and should blame politicians for selling out their trust of the people. No longer does anyone except perhaps some relatives and political associates hold politicians in high regard. That is why we need laws and regulations, to determine exactly what is to be allowed and what is not. You can and should blame corrupt politicians for selling out their trust of the people. They are committing overt crimes against the voters of these United States. Politics and Crime have become two faces of the same coin. Unfortunately, in the United States it has become coin of the realm.

Sources

http://www.americanchronicle.com/articles/534-- Illegal Aliens and Immigration, June 3, 2005

http://www.americanchronicle.com/articles/613-- All Immigration problems Solved, June 11, 2005

http://www.americanchronicle.com/articles/2884-- Labor Arbitrage? Better Known as Cheap Labor, October 12, 2005

http://www.americanchronicle.com/articles/3693 -- Coin of the Realm, November 14, 2005

This Page Intentionally Blank

Chapter 11 Mexifornia: A Phenomenon

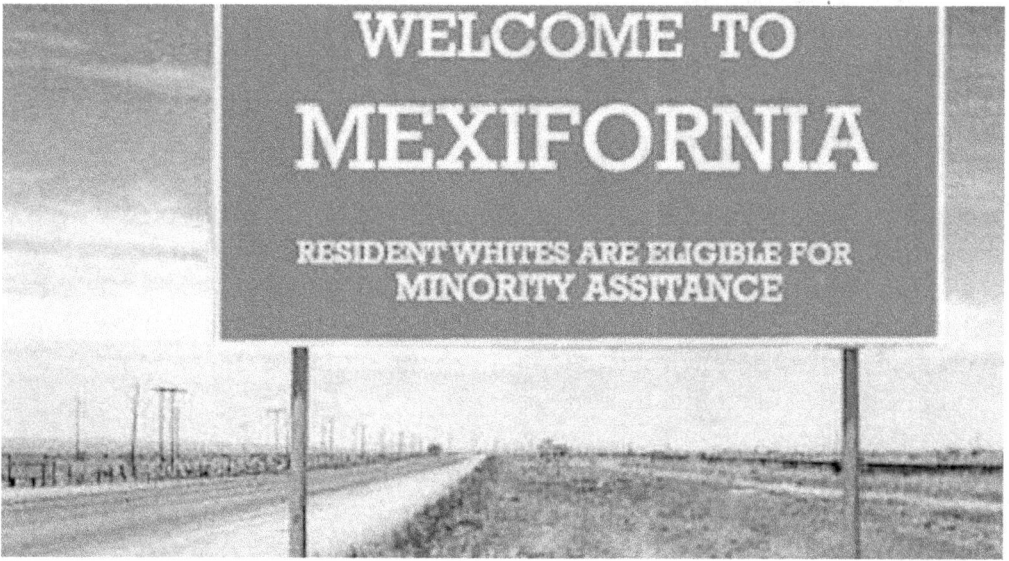

WELCOME TO
MEXIFORNIA
RESIDENT WHITES ARE ELIGIBLE FOR
MINORITY ASSITANCE

Victor Davis Hanson was born September 5, 1953. If there is a topic of interest in American politics, more than likely you have read something insightful about it that was written by this prolific writer. He is an American classicist, military historian, columnist and also a farmer. He has been a commentator on modern and ancient warfare and contemporary politics for National Review, The Washington Times and other media outlets. Today, we often see Victor Davis Hanson on Fox News offering his analysis and comments about Trump, immigration, and other topics. Rush Limbaugh frequently cites his work when making a special point.

At the turn of the 21st century, Hanson wrote a book which is read regularly by those wanting insights into the Mexification of California. His book is titled: *"Mexifornia: A State of Becoming.* Mexifornia is a new nickname for California, viewed as increasingly Mexican in population and culture, especially due to illegal immigration. There are a number of book reviews on Mexifornia. In this chapter, I rely on a number of notions presented in a book report / analysis written by Kevin Lamb.

As you know, there is a lot of fuss today over building a border wall, which should be a natural thing for a sovereign nation but because of

Democrats isn't for the US. Despite the vacillation about a border wall by Democrats, it seems obvious to most Americans that a border barricade is essential to peaceably maintain this sovereign nation. We know that for many years there has been massive illegal immigration from Mexico and South American Countries into California and other US border states. Today, the interlopers are coming in caravans of thousands and the situation is worse than ever.

Victor Davis Hanson who grew up in California, writes, "coupled with a loss of confidence in the old melting pot model of transforming newcomers into Americans, is changing the very nature of state. Yet we Californians have been inadequate in meeting this challenge, both failing to control our borders with Mexico and to integrate the new alien population into our mainstream."

His fifteen-year-old book has been refreshed since the original but whichever version you choose to read, you will find that it is part history, part political analysis, and part memoir. Hanson as noted, is often credited with the creation of the term "Mexifornia," but it may very well have been coined by another scholar in another time. One immediately knows its meaning without ever having to hear a formal definition.

The book is an intensely personal work by one of America's most important writers. Hanson is perhaps known best for his military histories and especially his social commentary about America and its response to terror after 9/11. But he is also a fifth-generation Californian who runs a family farm in the Central Valley and has written eloquent elegies for the decline of the small farm such as "Fields Without Dreams" and "The Land Was Everything." Hanson knows how it was and he knows how it is and without his acknowledgment, I am proud to have his words in this book.

Like these books, "Mexifornia" is an intensely personal look at what has changed in California over the last quarter century. In this case, however, Hanson's focus is on how not only California, the Southwest, and indeed how the entire nation has been affected by America's hemorrhaging borders and how those hurt worst are the Mexican immigrants themselves.

A large part of the problem, Hanson believes, comes from the opportunistic coalition that stymies immigration reform and, even worse, stifles an honest discussion of a growing problem. Conservative corporations, contractors, and agribusiness demand cheap wage labor from Mexico, whatever the social consequences. Meanwhile, "progressive" academics, journalists, government bureaucrats, and La Raza advocates envision illegal aliens as a vast new political constituency for those committed to the notion that victimhood, not citizenship, is the key to advancement.

What is Hispanic?

Let's stop a second here and define the term Hispanic as we all know its use today. Once upon a time there was no catch-all term for those south of the US/Mexican border down to the bottom of South America. Now there is a term, an unnatural term that sounds very natural—Hispanic, as if it comes from Old Hispania.

We owe the government for this well-used word. The US government desperately needed a way to be able to provide a checkbox so that certain people who have a certain description would be able to be treated differently from, if not better than others in the US. Yes, that about explains its purpose.

Calling everybody south of the Rio_Grande *Mexican* did not cut it and other attempts were just as ill conceived. Then, in 1975, along came Grace Flores-Hughes. She was a 26-year-old Latina working for the Department of Health, Education and Welfare in D.C. The Washington Post reported that she and a diverse group of federal employees, came together to convene as part of the Ad Hoc Committee on Racial and Ethnic Definitions.

Aside from figuring out what to call the Latinx community, they also touched on other "offensive" terms the U.S. had used, including "colored" and "Oriental." One might suggest that this committee was formed to help define politically correct v politically incorrect terminology. Yes, Virginia, the US government created political correctness.

"'Hispanic' was a term better than anything I had been called as a kid," Yet, the Latinx community did not like it. Flores-Huges — a Republican who currently sits on the National Hispanic Advisory Council for Trump— told The Washington Post in 2003; as a kid, she said, she was often called a "wetback" and a "dirty Mexkin."

However, despite a good term, several Latinx members of the committee did not agree with using the word "Hispanic." Instead, they wanted to go with "Latino" instead. So, labeling somebody who is Irish as a Mick or a Harp or a Moor would not do it either.

So, to this day, Pew Research shows that "11 percent of American adults with 'Hispanic' ancestry still do not identify as Hispanic." But, the term has stuck, for good or for bad. Created by the government for the bean counters, Hispanic has no real lovers.

The problems Hanson identifies in his book of foreign nationals coming at will unlawfully into the US by crossing the border with Mexico and arriving in California, has reached critical mass in California. However, it affects also those Americans who inhabit "Mexizona," "Mexichusetts" and other states of "becoming."

Hanson writes wistfully about his own growing up in the Central Valley of California when he was one of a handful of non-Hispanics in his elementary school and when his teachers saw it as their mission to give all students, Hispanic and "white" alike, a passport to the American Dream.

He continues to follow the fortunes of Hispanic friends he has known all his life--how they have succeeded in America and how they regard the immigration crisis. But if "Mexifornia" is emotionally generous at the strength and durability of the groups that have made California strong, it is also an indictment of the policies that got California into its present mess. But in the end, Hanson strongly believes that our traditions of assimilation, integration, and intermarriage may yet remedy a problem that the politicians and ideologues have allowed to get out of hand. But, even Hanson does not have the answer for "when?"

Many of us remember California's gubernatorial recall election during the almost turn of the century period in which Hanson wrote his book. The "re-election" highlighted a number of crucial issues facing the residents of California, which most of us know is our nation's most populated state—a very important state in many ways.

Due to major mismanagement of officials in the Sacramento Capitol, California at the time had a $38-billion budget deficit; a financially bloated and deteriorating educational system; a tripling of the state's car tax; an energy crisis aggravated by inept regulatory mismanagement; an overburdened health-care system; a state that issued driver's licenses to illegal aliens, and it also granted in-state college tuition costs to illegal aliens.

The burner on this for the *"Other 49,"* is that its largesse for foreigners did not extend to other US states. California charges out-of-state tuition fees for legal residents of other states. California as a state is not well liked by other states for these and lots of other valid reasons. It is not that the "Other 49" have an exe to grind, it is that California knows how to stiff its neighboring states and the rest of the country. That is why the "Other 49" would be Calexit YES in a big way.

Many of us know illegal foreign nationals who reside in California and other states. We know their neighbors and friends also. Illegal foreign nationals work cheap as domestics for a lot of citizens and they get close to each other because of that relationship. So the Americans that tell us they love the new illegal foreign interlopers gain by paying them insufficient wages and find it very nice that they receive great work and smiles from the people who behind the scenes are afraid of the shadows of their illegal-ness. Who does this really help?

Actually, and it is not the theme of this book but it is true nonetheless, I have solved the problem with 60 million illegal interlopers in America several times. The synopsis book on this subject is called *How to End DACA, Sanctuary Cities, & Resident Illegal Aliens.* The subtitle is *"This is the best solution to wipe out all the shadows in America."* The Amazon URL is https://www.amazon.com/dp/1947402617. If we all want to recognize the problem and provide an America-first solution, this book is the ticket to that end. Yes, I wrote it so I know.

The media's coverage of these issues (as one usually expects) tends to dwell upon superficial features (personalities and anecdotal accounts), which often leave the impression that these matters are disjointed problems. Put simply, journalists are reluctant to recognize a common causal relationship between the state's simmering political, social and economic upheaval and California's shifting demographic population base. There are few members of the press who are not registered Democrats and who do not take their marching orders directly from the Democrat leadership.

For obvious liberal and egalitarian reasons, the "mainstream" press (as promoters of "multicultural diversity") selectively avoids connecting the dots hence, as a "nation of immigrants," and they suggest that it is right that America should continue to indefinitely absorb the flow of legal and illegal migrants—as long as they are not dumped by Trump on their particular sanctuary city.

Those without jobs because an illegal has the job often do not get to speak to the press. The egalitarian press believes that the "benefits" of "cultural enrichment" will easily outweigh financial costs to the poor citizens and to the state.

In other words, what does the state's budget deficits, educational, welfare and health-care costs, traffic congestion, water shortages, pollution and environmental burdens have to do with the state's demographically expanding and changing population base? For illegal interlopers, they believe the philosophy must be "Let them come and the assimilation process -- with the right mix of government policies -- will work itself out." Of course, nobody in the excellency rankings should have to chip in to pay for the new residents whose poor jobs give them hardly enough to survive.

This sort of thinking is endemic and it shows how the media and cultural elites continue to view this seemingly disparate matrix of political, social, economic and cultural indicators: legal and illegal immigration levels simply have a negligible adverse impact on the average native Californian. In other words, the big shots with the money and power do not care at all about the rest.

Really accurate and painstaking studies would prove these premises false as nobody gains when sub minimum age workers from any source take anybody's jobs. If subminimum wage work were desirable in America, I posit that there would no minimum wage. Who would need a union to grab them a sub-par minimum wage?

Because people are starving and they see American citizens, in better straits than they, why not take what you cannot earn? I see that as the mentality of the illegal interloper after watching people eat a lot better than they do in the US.

Consequently, crime rates are disproportionately higher in certain neighborhoods, not because of the presence of violent Hispanic gang members, but because of the state's overall higher unemployment rate. Everybody has to eat even if you get your grass cut for lots less by illegal interlopers than the going rate.

Welfare costs to all Californians and Americans in general are increasing, not because of the presence of more low-wage, low-skill Mexican immigrants, but because the state's minimum wage and sub-minimum wage work opportunities fail to cover the costs of single-parents struggling to raise a family on a low-wage salary. Knowing this, one would think California would shut off the many spigots from which illegal interlopers flow. Yet, Sacramento has its own reasons for keeping life as it is. Maybe it helps them get re-elected? What a shame!

Traffic congestion in the whole state is worse than ever, not because more people are driving more cars and thus clogging up highways, but because the state fails to spend more on highway construction when usage is up. Giving illegal foreign nationals drivers licenses makes them feel they are citizens that should be denied nothing and their use of highways and byways is unlimited by their immigration status. They add to the highway burden so California should bee ready to pay but it is not ready.

What compounds this perplexing mindset is captured in Victor Davis Hanson's book *Mexifornia: A State of Becoming.* As a classicist at California State University (Fresno) and fifth-generation Central Valley farmer, Hanson brings to the table an interesting background -- the insights of a scholar steeped in history, language and culture combined with the experience of an agricultural farmer who has first-hand experience in witnessing his hometown of Selma transformed from a "unicultural" community to a Hispanic-dominated enclave.

How'd that happen and was it good or expected? Hanson has the insights now to teach us all from the perfect mix one would expect in terms of providing a first-rate analysis of the implications of California's ethnic transformation into something else. Who knows what?

A book reviewer might say that "While he seems to grasp the fact captured in the words of the Pretenders' song –'my city was gone' – this particular reviewer thinks "Hanson seems nearly delusional in attempting to explain this phenomenon: ethnicity and demographic factors are, in his view, irrelevant when it comes to understanding how California communities have changed." As smart as he is, I think Mr. Hanson suffers a bit from having read "On Walden Pond."

The problem in California is one of permissiveness of process fostered by a group of no-mind buffoons in Sacramento -- simply allowing assimilation to work. What if it doesn't? With no *thumping uncle* to make the nephews do as they are supposed to do, why should they do anything that is positive for anybody else?

Illegal immigrants know they run the show because they run the show. Too bad America! They refuse to assimilate because the thumping uncle is not there to make them assimilate. So, they turned a once successful melting pot into a balkanized cauldron—not because of who they are and what they represent, but because of a host of other reasons (cultural, social, and economic barriers) in which Western values and norms have failed to take root. Once permitted to live normally as an illegal alien, the world became their oyster. Once given, don't even think of taking it away.

Victor Davis Hanson is no slouch but he does have a major kind streak, which can be a fault when clear signals are needed.

The book reviewer I have cited is not necessarily a Hanson fan. He sees Hanson's explanations for his conclusions in what he refers to as a slim 150-page volume as less than convincing. As political scientist James Q. Wilson noted, "Mexifornia is less a book than an expanded magazine article." And since it contains no footnotes, references, bibliography or index, Hanson essentially wedges undocumented facts, assertions and statistics between anecdotes. Tipping his hand, he stated in a recent National Review article, "objective data cannot tell us whether a front-line state like California is saved or lost because of illegal immigration."

The reviewer continues: "What is baffling about Hanson's book is that he seems to have his pulse on the symptoms of California's immigration problems, even to the extent that these are properly attributed to the nonstop flow of illegal immigration, but in the final analysis he fails to properly diagnose the causes which contribute to this dilemma of "assimilation."

For Hanson, the problem underlying the flight of illegal Mexicans into the U.S. is a despotic Mexican government that is exporting its undesirables (Mestizos and Indian underclass) northward beyond the country's border." Of course those in America who are hurt more than Hanson may have stronger opinions about the impact of the unbridled flow if illegal interlopers into America with nobody in the US Congress attempting to preserve American jobs. Show me one member of Congress for the American worker. I can find none!

"Hanson seems to recognize what is patently obvious: Mexican society -- from the government on down -- breeds corruption. The question he tiptoes around is: What makes it so comparatively corrupt? He argues that the heart of California's immigration problem is "complex," and this complexity is reflected in a lack of "domestic" reforms on the part of the Mexican government, reinforced by U.S. foreign policies toward Mexico that will force an end to its "tribalism" and "class" discrimination."

"Once reforms take hold in Mexico, minimizing and reversing government corruption, then the conditions will be ripe to diminish the northward flow of illegal immigrants." Really?

"For any sophisticated reader with commonsense, the frustration boils down to this: Only someone of this intellectual caliber can miss something so strikingly obvious. Some points that Hanson raises seem to abruptly dodge the logical extension of his reasoning. Other positions strike a bizarre degree of inconsistency He describes the deplorable conditions that have turned his hometown into a Third World community as the small community turned largely Hispanic, then expresses his personal admiration for the contributions of Latino culture to America's diversity." Should we fight or abandon our property? A dilemma only if you hold no property.

Being a major fan of Victor Davis Hanson as a writer and political analyst, I hate to see the pot shots from the book review and others who see his analysis as well off the wall. But, I admit there is more remorse provided and perhaps not enough, than there is a set of solutions that can be employed for Americans to win the day. I'd ask Mr. Hanson to talk to more others before he makes his next set of conclusions.

I do love Hanson's firm belief in the "melting pot" metaphor. So long as Mexican immigrants are properly assimilated into the grain of American culture, then America benefits from this ethno-cultural integration. But, they are not integrating. Having read more than Hanson for years, I agree that Victor Davis Hanson in his book fails to adequately address the alternative possibilities.

Hanson might accept that some cultures are simply unassimilable or incompatible with the cultural standards, norms and traditions of the majority population. Suppose, even more significantly, it were found that some immigrant cultures are assimilable only up to a point. Would that impact any set of recommendations forthcoming?

The reviewers say that what is missing from his analysis is any consideration of the law of averages. Let's look at some comments in this regard:

"If, on average, Latinos commit more violent crime than say non-Hispanic whites or Asians; if, on average, they rely upon state welfare services more than say other major California ethnic groups; if, on average, they depend on low-wage, low-skilled jobs; if, on average, they perform more poorly and score lower grades than other comparative ethnic groups, so on and so forth, then how will this impact the social and political landscape?

This can be viewed for what it realistically is, and to some extent Hanson seems to suggest that if current levels of illegal Latino immigration persist as projected to 2050 by census bureau estimates, the lack of low-skilled jobs could eventually lead to a Brazilian-style balkanized society increasingly divided by class, race, and ethnicity" Nobody wants this so we must not only think out of the box to solve the problem but we have to break out of the cushy Davis-Hanson box to free our minds to think rationally about it all.

"The situation is one in which these ethnic differences are likely to persist rather than dissolve in the great "melting pot." If so, native Californians are likely to either flee the state or seek refuge in areas of California that remain relatively insulated from the ghetto conditions associated with Latino-majority communities. Liberal politicians will seize on this development, seeking the ethnic-block vote of Latinos, denouncing their plight as victims of "racism" and "discrimination."

The Reviewers find positive things also in this book. To his credit, for example, "Hanson would reform our immigration system and limit the flow of illegal immigration into the U.S., even though he offers few specifics as to how he would accomplish this task. [He is a friend of the big and beautiful wall and this may be his solution].

"Since 9/11 which at the time of this book review, which I have referenced, was just two years prior, the leaders have replaced Daniel Patrick Moynihan as the neo-conservative's favorite liberal—he remains a registered Democrat, claims to be an old-fashioned liberal—but has managed to write 121 bylined articles for National Review and National Review Online in the past two years.

Humph! So what?

Hopefully, over time, the reviewers assert, Hanson will reassess some of these positions, shed the meaningless cliches of the "melting pot," and apply his first-rate historical insights toward a more sound resolution of California's demographic transformation before it is too late.

I hope that does not mean that Victor Davis Hanson will stop thinking. Maybe we have to love good people who want good things to find bad things in the writings of good people because it does not fit their fundamental ideas. Point is if it is not good for America, shed the idea.

Nobody agrees with everybody 100% of the time. I don't know that I would stake my life on a major opinion of Victor Davis Hanson but I would surely consider it and take more time than normal.

Mexifornia, if you are VDH, was his life. For me, it is not. I have friends in California who think America should roll open its borders for everybody simply because they had a good experience with one or several or many illegal interlopers who charged them little for their services..

Victor Davis Hanson is a good man. My cousin in California is a good man who employs illegal foreign nations as many do in California because they work cheap and they like him and they invite his family for real Mexican / South American food. Perhaps if they were working for minimum wage, these families would not invite them to their tables.

The bottom line is that California and Californians resent the National Authority of the Constitution and as the biggest bully state in the Union, many Californians think they should have whatever they want whether it is pro-American or not. I agree with Cal-Exit. Go get what you want California on your way out of America.

Go for it. I think having the selfish state of California out of the Union, the union would be stronger.

Thinking out loud, most of us know that there was a time, not so long ago, when we Americans understood that newcomers did not need to be taught in their own language in our schools. Even less did we believe that their children required special classes in ethnic pride or separate, race-based college graduation ceremonies.

It sickens me to think that there is a national lobbying group calling itself La Raza (The Race) which has slogans such as: "For La Raza everything; for those outside La Raza, nothing." If La Raza was for helping America, I would evaluate it but their words are shocking, even chilling. I am an American, period.

I believed in American civic education for immigrants, which, combined with intermarriage, integration and popular culture, led to rapid parity for those immigrants' children in terms of education, income and influence. Needless to say, in that earlier time, immigrants came to the U.S. from

Mexico and other countries largely under legal auspices and in measured numbers that did not overwhelm our once formidable powers of assimilation.

What we see going on with Caravan immigration today is a tragedy, and it is not simply a result of the federal government abdicating its responsibility to control our borders (although the federal government has certainly done precisely that). The citizens of California and others are also complicit in this tragedy. For instance, millions who used to cut our own lawns and clean our own houses now consider such tasks beneath us, as if America's middle class has embraced as its birthright the culture and leisure once confined to an aristocratic elite.

Suddenly our young people, our poor and our unskilled find jobs picking apples or laying tiles somehow demeaning. So-called dead-end jobs are no longer a rite of passage for our youth, but are deemed proper only for unskilled laborers from Mexico, whose toil, we are assured, keeps our produce, restaurants and hotels inexpensive.

Chapter 12 Is Illegal Immigration a Moral Notion?

If you have heat in your home in the US and your neighbor does not, is it OK if they bust your doors down one day and come in and settle in your livingroom? Then, if you allow it with no complaining; what next will you owe them for the privilege of being warm in your house?

If you have popcorn in your home in the US and your neighbor does not, is it OK if they bust your doors down one day and come in and eat your popcorn? Then, if you allow them to eat your popcorn, with no complaining, what next will you owe them for the privilege of being warm with a full bowl of popcorn in your house?

If you have lots of food in your home in the US and your neighbor does not, is it OK if they bust your doors down one day and come in and settle in your livingroom or kitchen to guzzle some of your finest victuals? Then, if you allow it with no complaining; what next will you owe them the next time for the privilege of eating for free in your house?

When does it stop?

If it were your neighbor, for most it would stop before they got in the first time unless you chose to help make them warm. But, if they were nasty neighbors, it might never get that far.

The point is that in America, what's yours is your and what is mine is mine. An interloper who crosses the border and wants to take yours just because they want it has no claim and just like your neighbor, you would and should rebuff them.

Is it right to get in the habit of talking about illegal immigration in economic rather than in moral terms? Who knows? Who is breaking into whom's home town or whose home?

There are many interlopers who are happy with Americans doing the heavy lifting and they do no lifting. Consider the situation from a moral perspective. Do we really expect hard-working illegal youths from central Mexico to work 30 years in construction, hotels, or the fields without marrying, having children, losing jobs or getting hurt? Think about it.

Is that a real question and to whom is it asked? If it were asked to me, I would answer "no way." Stay home. We did not ask you to come. Do not come. I believe that youths from Central Mexico or Central America willing to work in the US for 30 years in construction, hotels or the fields without marrying, having children, losing jobs or getting hurt, should check out the probabilities of that happening anywhere in the world-- including staying at home.

I think if you are not invited specifically into the US, you should not come. If you come, assess the risks and do not blame the gracious American people for any of your failings. Nobody asked you to come.

How can such workers—without legal status, education or mastery of English—support a family on $10 an hour when most native Americans can't do so on $20? Will we continue to shrug and say, "At least the money is better than in Mexico," or, "None of our own people will do the work," or, "They are going to drive anyway, so let's give them driver's licenses"—all the easy platitudes that justify the current chaos?

No sir. I say either go back if it is not good enough because you are not invited. Or endure it and try to gain recognition in this country for your goodness and not for your demands.

Unemployment is high and rising in California, but we are told that even more illegal workers from Mexico are needed. Not so! Can it really be the case that the free market can no longer operate to attract American workers through rising wages—even assuming an absence of a pool of unskilled labor? We know that there are many liars everywhere. An unskilled Mexican or SA worker lowers the wages for all. Stay home please, and keep wages higher in the US for all. Work on correcting the ills in your own country.

Meanwhile, many who ought to know better, champion the employer's right to hire whomever he chooses, and assure us that Mexican immigration poses no more of a problem for the U.S. than nineteenth century Italian immigration. One cannot believe that they are unaware that multiculturalism did not exist in our schools in the nineteenth century, that we do not share an adjacent open border with Italy, and that Italian immigrants did not flood our country unlawfully as part of the national caravan strategy of the Italian government. Great thought but it is not reflective of what is happening.

We are told that blanket amnesty and a grant of legal status will ensure assimilation and prosperity. It did not happen after the 1986 Reagan amnesty so why should it happen now? Statistics suggest that after 20 years, even legal Mexican immigrants have double the welfare rates of American citizens.

In one study, students surveyed at 13 years of age and then again at 17 were 50 percent more likely at 17 to identify themselves as "Mexicans" as opposed to "Mexican-Americans"—this despite, or perhaps even because of, having spent four years in American high schools. If they are never going to like US, they should not come and surely, they should not be admitted to our country. It is not theirs.

Almost every well-intended and enlightened gesture designed to help immigrants over the last three decades—bilingual education, ever expanding and new state welfare programs, the affirmation of a hyphenated identity and the radical historical revisionism of southwestern American history—has been detrimental to the processes of assimilation and economic improvement.

Almost everything stern and uncompromising that for two centuries has helped other immigrants to the United States—entry under legal auspices, language immersion, autonomy from government assistance, rapid assumption of an American identity and eager acceptance of mainstream American culture—has either been dismissed as passé or carried on halfheartedly. The new guys simply are not interested in being Americans. Let them go home sooner rather than later.

Most Californians of all backgrounds understand the growing social and cultural costs that flow from this intolerable situation. Yet the Orwellian alliance of many libertarian-leaning conservatives—who embrace the idea of a perpetual supply of hard-working, unskilled and inexpensive workers—with the race industry of the Left—which envisions an endless influx of unassimilated potential voters, who can be appealed to on the basis of group rather than individual identity—tends to demonize any discussion of the issue. You can't even broach the subject with a Democrat.

Embittered Californians give tacit approval to therapeutic bromides in their schools and state agencies—and then flock to the polls to vent their rage by voting to end what they see as special consideration for those who broke the law in coming here.

In the last decade, California majorities have voted against state aid to illegal immigrants, affirmative action and bilingual education, but far fewer than a majority will admit to taking part. It is not a healthy thing to have a voting population of millions thinking privately what they won't express publicly.

Mexico, a richly endowed but nearly failed state, with 31 billionaires who like to keep their money, continues to refuse to do the political, cultural and economic restructuring that is needed to turn itself around. Indeed, why should it bother making these reforms when it can export potential dissidents from its hinterland to the U.S., gaining in the process $12 billion in remittances from expatriates? (These remittances constitute the second largest source of foreign exchange to the Mexican economy.) Not only that, but as noted previously, Mexico finds that the longer its expatriates stay away from Mexico and in the U.S., the more they come to love Mexico.

Unintended Consequences

Illustrating the law of unintended consequences, today's illegal immigration crisis was not quite what any of the stakeholders in this immigration had anticipated. In addition to its cheap labor, tax-conscious business interests are responsible for masses of unassimilated residents who eventually plugged into the state's near-bankrupt entitlement industry. In addition to a larger bloc vote, the pro-labor Left discovered that the wages of its own impoverished domestic constituencies were eroded by the influx of less expensive and more industrious alien workers. Yes, the facts indicate that the new guys will work cheaper than those who think they belong.

A full 50 percent of real wage labor losses was recently attributed by the Labor Department to the influx of cheap immigrant labor. While we continue to import this labor, millions of second-generation Hispanic and other legal laborers are making not much more than the minimum wage.

Of course, few of the professors and politicians who support illegal immigration—whether for continuance of cheap labor or for the sake of the entitlement industries—live in California's new apartheid communities like Orange Cove, Mendota or Parlier, communities where Mexican immigrants make up the vast majority of the population and struggle with dismal schools, high crime, little revenue and other social problems akin to those in Mexico.

In a time of war, under the threat of domestic terrorism and with their state budget tens of billions of dollars in the red, Californians are predictably restive and looking for answers. They cannot quite figure out how a state with Hollywood, the Silicon Valley, vast industrial and manufacturing sectors, great ports, timber, oil, tourism, a vast agricultural industry, an ideal climate—not to mention some of the nation's highest sales and income taxes—is broken and paralyzed with billions of dollars in annual deficit.

They are considering what kind of future they want. In more placid times, this could be an academic exercise. Under current circumstances, it is an urgent necessity. Sacramento, unfortunately, has lost is ears.

In the end, the immigration crisis is simple to understand, but it can also seem to involve an unsolvable calculus. Californians want a lot of their work done cheaply by illegal immigrants who, they wrongly assume, will transform themselves quickly into Americans who have been trined to enjoy low wages.

In turn, too many downtrodden Mexicans and their elite American advocates romanticize Mexico, a nation that has brought them misery and driven them to flight, and deprecate the U.S., which gave them sanctuary.

In a country where there may be anywhere from eight to fifteen million illegal immigrants, or perhaps as many as 60 million as your author Brian W. Kelly asserts and proves in this books, is there any hope for avoiding the nightmare of Balkanization? Perhaps.

After all, California got into its present mess only during the last 30 years, and then only by doing almost everything wrong. Electing Democrats is the first scourge on the many scourges to failure.

Thus we need not do everything right, but we must simply return to what we used to do so well: insist that immigration be measured and legal, do more of our own unpleasant work, enforce all of our laws equally, emphasize assimilation and return to thinking and speaking of Americans as individuals rather than in terms of their racial or group identities.

Amen! Build the wall

California does not want America's help in becoming a better state. Thus, the *Other 49* are happy to say *Sayonara* even if they cannot speak any other Japanese. If California does not want the "Trump" wall or any wall, then, America should destroy the wall between California and Mexico.

Let California have what it wants – a Mexifornia more like a Mesicofornia with no allegiance to the US. America and Americans should permit this and in fact, encourage California's secession—Calexit. Maybe there is so much change in the secession idea on the table that California can solve all its issues. By being separated from America, it is clear that America itself will have a better chance for long-term survival.

Chapter 13 The Demise of California

https://www.sierrabooster.com/latest-news/demise-of-california 4/16/2018

California is turning to Democrats for answers but just as Detroit has received no answers from Democrats neither has California. The best things Democrats do in California is dupe the voters into voting Democrat. They are very good at that for sure. Each election, more Dems take office and things get worse; just like Detroit. Democrats are winners because they use the "lie" as a major weapon even though most Americans do not believe in lies. Americans actually believe Democrats are telling the truth.

Nobody thanks Republicans even when thanks is due. It took eight years for Republicans to shepherd Detroit through a bankruptcy caused by inept Democrat leadership for 100 years. Republicans brought about Detroit's economic revival. Ingrate Democrats are expected to win big this election in Michigan. The people forget.

One can say in California's heyday, the Republicans were in charge but now, only in a few counties such as Sierra, do the Republicans of today get any votes at all. And, the basket weavers have taken notice suggesting California has gone to hell in a handbasket. It is cause and effect. Democrats no longer think of the people first.

Voter turnout has been falling in all of California for years, but that's not the case in the conservative northeastern part of the state where Dr. Rob Martinelli's article was recently published. In rural Sierra County, more than 85 percent of eligible voters are registered. And they cast their ballots, too -- usually for Republicans.

We can thank Dr. Ron Martinelli for most of the thoughts in this chapter. It is not presented exactly as he originally wrote but the essence of the demise of California is right here in this chapter. I would say Martinelli would agree with most of what is in this book and he could have written it himself. I like how he turns a phrase and so there is a lot of the good Doctor written in this chapter.

Recently, he wrote an excellent, but sad article on the demise of California. I have used the article as the basis for this chapter about what has gone wrong with California. As we get close to putting this book into the history logs, I include these excerpts and this perspective to remind the reader that *Hasta La Vista California* means exactly that.

And, dear California, you may put your sweet lips a little closer to the phone and go ahead and pretend that you're the one state, all alone. I'll tell Sacramento to turn their rhetoric way down low and you can tell the rest of the country you'll have to go—please! Please go! Martinelli is the author between the quotes.

"I sit in the LAX terminal after concluding business in downtown Los Angeles for the past two days, I cannot help but reflect upon my journey from once a California native to a new resident of the Great State of Texas and why. You see, in my personal and professional opinion, the once great State of California has in essence become a third world country."

I hope all Californians heard that before it is too late to turn your big ship around. Humph! Third World Country – "The concept of the "third world" has evolved to describe countries that suffer from low economic development, high levels of poverty and little to no ability to utilize natural or economic resources."

That is according to French demographer Alfred Sauvey, from way back in1952 but it surely applies.

"While the reasons for California's ever-spiraling downwards status from 1st World economic prominence and prosperity to near 3rd World malaise are many; I will assert that when you combine uber-liberal politicians, with rich elitist Hollywood Celebrities, dotcom CEO billionaires, disengaged millennials and illegal aliens; you in effect create the circumstances where your city or state becomes a 3rd World environment."

"The process of California's demise from the "Golden State" to 3rd World status has been slow but steady; supported and enabled by the aforementioned actors."

Many of these new kinds of actors live in Sacramento. They're bad actors for sure.

"While much of the legislated changes for the worse have been designed and voted in by politicians in Sacramento; municipal politicians and a complicit uninformed, naive and entitled voting public must also share blame. After all, when 51% of those on some type of government subsidy out-vote the 49% of the money earning and tax paying citizenry, any state is doomed to failure. With California now a "Sanctuary State" and their "libtard" Democratic state legislature pushing for voting rights for illegal aliens, the state will never recover. My thoughts exactly. California is finished."

Like an alcoholic who chooses not to recover, California will continue to have that one more drink until there are no parts left that are not already long gone.

"My observations during my short visit to Los Angeles underscored many of the problems Californians are facing as they follow like lemmings their Governor Jerry "Moonbeam" Brown, their Democratic legislators and urban mayors like Eric Garretti off the economic cliff."

"Literally nothing substantive is good about L.A. An ever-growing homeless subculture populates the downtown area. The intoxicated, drug influenced, mentally impaired and criminals are everywhere. They literally surround Civic Center, federal buildings and courts – the so-called foundations and protectors of the Rule of Law and society. How ironic to be surrounded by the failures these very systems, liberal politicians and judges have created. Isn't karma interesting to watch in real time?"

"The homeless, numbering in the thousands, sleep in the shadows of immense, gleaming edifices owned by multi-billion-dollar international conglomerates and dotcom corporations. Business executives in Brioni suits and workers quickly pass by the unwashed masses, while holding their noses to screen out the stench of urine and feces. The obvious health and safety hazards to the public are too many to count."

"Interconnecting Los Angeles city roadways and state highways designed to transport the commuting, tax paying public to their job sites are a debacle. The ribbons of roadways are a mess of potholed, weed infested, trash laden, graffiti vandalized passages filled with vehicles lined up bumper-to-bumper going nowhere fast. These are your tax dollars at work. While California voters grumble and groan, in the end they just seem to accept their fate as one of the prices to pay for living the California dream."

Then, in the next election rather than cast blame on leaders, they vote in Democrat majorities again.

"You see, the working public has no time to get out and protest the outrageous and constant increases in taxes on gas, municipal services, vehicle registrations, rapid transit and a bullet train going to nowhere. Only the unemployed, government subsidized masses have time to demonstrate in the streets to ensure that their subsidies continue. Since the liberal politicians in Sacramento know this dynamic and their power base all too well, the taxation without representation continues."

"I was staying at a hotel near LAX and my mileage commute to downtown L.A. was a mere twelve miles. However, it took me every bit of one hour and twenty minutes to arrive at my destination. I then paid

$20 for the privilege of parking my car in a public lot. Of course, this was after I paid $30 a day to park my rental car at my hotel. Nice. I'm seriously considering Uber next time."

"Since I frequently travel throughout California on business, I will tell you that Los Angeles is a mirror image of all of the other large urban cities in the state. I have observed similar and even worse depressed and dysfunctional urban environments in the San Francisco Bay Area, Orange County, San Diego and a number of other cities."

California is rapidly becoming a two-tiered society of the very rich and the very poor, similar to the 2nd and 3rd World countries I regularly visit. The middle class, small business owners and the retired are either being pushed out of state and/or escaping in droves to such tax free, business friendly and less crime ridden states such as Nevada, Arizona, Texas and Florida. Lame duck Gov. Moonbeam and the state's liberal Democratic legislature know this. New Governor Newsom, another Democrat knows it too! They just don't care because their power base is now assured. Just ask any of their castrated, powerless Republican colleagues

"There will never again be a Republican administration in California. The days of Ronald Reagan have long passed. The candidates lining up for the governor's race in 2018 are Open Borders and Sanctuary State advocates Anthony Villaraigosa and Lt. Governor Gavin Newsom. Governor Brown and his Democratic legislature are pulling out all the stops creating legislation that will allow illegal aliens in the state to vote in state and local elections. Republicans, conservatives and moderates don't stand a chance."

"Here are just some of things Californian's have done in recent years to turn their state into a 3rd World mess. Passed Proposition 47 which has since freed tens of thousands of felons from state prisons and county jails back into communities. Prop. 47 also eviscerated the parole enforcement agency and created a system where police on the streets can't even enforce outstanding felony and misdemeanor warrants anymore."

"Police no longer arrest people for being under the influence of dangerous drugs. What would be the point; it's just a misdemeanor. They have reduced the crime of auto theft to a citable misdemeanor. Steal a car; get caught and get a ticket. Commit non-violent crimes, get arrested and you are out the same day with a promise to appear in court that will not ever be enforced. No warrant enforcement, remember? Amazing!"

"California's new "Sanctuary State" status supports and enables its Open Borders mentality. Police in a number of cities such as San Francisco, Oakland and Los Angeles are ordered not to assist ICE with border enforcement. Remember the Kate Steinle murder case where her five-time convicted criminal and deported illegal alien was acquitted? Well, that's the political mentality that created that circumstance. This is also an excellent example that liberal politicians in California are willing to sacrifice the innocent to demonstrate that they support violent illegal alien criminals."

"What happens in California's larger cities filters down to its medium and small sized cities as well. I recently wrote about the city of Salinas, CA that experienced an incredible 150% increase in its homicide rate from 2014 – 2015. Salinas rated as one of the nation's 30 most violent cities. Fifty percent of all of their murders were gang and drug related, with the predominate gang members being illegal aliens. I can only wonder how Silicon Valley dot-commers' who are paying over half a million bucks for a home and commute over four hours a day to San Jose like living in that violent environment?"

"Which brings me back to why my successful business owner wife and I escaped to Texas. The state loves us. No commute problems, no state taxes and we live in an area where there is little to no crime. Our area just outside of San Antonio some of the best school districts in the U.S.; high employment, great people and lots of fun things to do."

"My wife and I live a great life on a ranch with a river in our backyard where we can fish, swim, kayak and BBQ with family and neighbors anytime we want. The price? Less than you would pay for a one-bedroom studio condo in any of the cities in California I've mentioned. New home buyers only need three percent down to purchase a home and veterans make no down payments. If you are a younger middle-classer, a small business owner or retired, you'd be nuts to remain in California."

"With California over a trillion dollars in debt and 30% of their budget going to subsidizing illegal aliens at the expense of hard-working, taxpayers who have little to no voice on how their state is run, the state and the majority of their citizens are doomed. That's what a two-tiered society eventually creates . One heck of a THIRD WORLD COUNTRY!"

"The truth is blatantly obvious... and yet the left STILL turns a blind eye.. I say let this Titanic sink...."

"People need to wake up, and it's too bad you won't be forwarding this to your left-leaning, closed-minded, egalitarian friends for fear of their reprisals!"

This article had twenty-eight comments at the time I read it at https://www.sierrabooster.com/latest-news/demise-of-california. I have taken the liberty to include these comments below. The sierrabooster.com organization and your author are on the same page in terms of opening up America's eyes as to the big problem in California and how it must be solved before it affects the rest of the country in a negative way. My thanks to this group for their kindness and vigilance.

Comments

28 Comments in web site sequence.
Name used and date of comment provided.
A few comments have been edited for punctuation.

Elmer A. Omohundro Jr.
6/20/2018 10:06:40 pm

You have published the truth as I've lived it having been born in Altadena, CA, 88 years ago next month. I remember the influx of undocumented aliens in Los Angeles who over-ran the schools, hospitals, emergency services, hospitals, and other public institutions, causing many to close and go bankrupt. Ronald Reagan tried his best to keep the State going, but the Democrats were too aligned with the Socialists. The Governorship of the Brown Administration has led the state toward bankruptcy. But, what can we expect when the public votes against a "train to nowhere" and the Governor ignores their wishes placing the public in debt for over 50 years. I won't be around to see it, but my Great, Great, Grandchildren will be. How sad.

Roland E. Otte
7/9/2018 03:19:28 am

I have seldom read a better written piece. Bravo Dr. Martinelli.

Dan Wheeler
7/13/2018 05:14:54 pm

Like the author of this piece I too also escaped from the Democratic People's Republic.

After 19 years as a contractor I got fed up with the regulations, workmans comp costs, idiot brain dead building inspectors, taxes I too fled to Texas. I knew there would be no way we could retire there.

And as the author stated I too one time had a two hour drive from SLAC Stanford to San Jose Airport a distance of 30-odd miles.

As many articles have said it is only a matter of time till California is no more because eventually you run out of other people's money!

Thomas E. Porter
7/16/2018 03:17:23 pm

I agree. Unfortunately my spouse of 56 years wants to be near her granddaughter. I am originally from a town near the Okla-Tex border and have a brother and couple of sisters living in TX.

Further, I find the people in TX much friendlier and genuine. Should anything happen to my wife, Heaven forbid, I will be out of here quicker than a cat can lick it's butt.   Thanks for the article.

Steven Hammond
8/2/2018 11:02:10 am

This state has gone downhill ever since Jerry Brown was in office I don't know why he can't be impeached for putting California residents safety Last and putting all the criminals first and if Newsom gets in, the state will get worse and worse and worse and if that happens though I love California, I'm not going to stay in California.

Isn't it a nice thing to do to go watch somebody go to the bathroom in San Francisco. It's going to cost over 17 million dollars for them to clean the city up annually what can we do with that type of money other than cleaning up after the drug addicts that are given free syringes made of plastic but they want to ban straws. This mentality escapes me and like I said all they want to do is put our safety Last.

How could they have been voted in office? We need to change to make California great again and we cannot let people like these leaders ruin our lives and livelihood and keep us all in constant Danger. So, think about that when you go to the polls this year have a great day God bless you all

Albo
8/11/2018 03:56:24 pm

Why can't Brown be impeached? It used to be just the Leftist ideology of the elites that implemented idiocy for everyone but themselves, which destroyed the schools, families, safety, jobs. But now the reason is that it's a fixed game; i.e., the whole political structure is truly ossified, with no alternative voices to the Democrats in politics.

It's killed social mobility and a path to fix things. Just like in the Third World. Mostly, we are becoming Latin America, which is corrupt and without opportunity.

Gordon Steele
8/6/2018 06:36:05 pm

As Canadians, we have always enjoyed our many trips to California. We feel it is a wonderful place and superior to all other places in the USA we have visited. Sure the freeways in LA are crowded, but they are an excellent road system allowing more people than in all of Canada to get from place to place. You must be a Trump supporter!

Steve McKeown
8/10/2018 08:59:55 pm

And you obviously support that spineless pretty boy socialist Trudeau. Feel free to visit California any time you like. Although your opinion might change the first time you and your family are attacked by MS-13 gang members.

Donnalink
8/16/2018 12:13:40 pm

Gordon Steele; There is a saying, "No one knows what goes on behind closed doors". When you live the day to day atrocities that are destroying the State, the experience is quite different from a drive-by view. For you it is a closed door view. In other words, unreal!

Susie Torres
11/4/2018 09:09:55 am

Visiting California and living in California are two very different experiences, with absolutely no comparison. Our freeways are one thing, but they have no positive impact on the quality of life for hard working, tax paying citizens. Visitors who have never lived in California see our state from a completely different perspective, which has nothing to do with the realities of living here.

Do we have great weather, absolutely, but now a days there are far more negative things that impact every-day living than the positive of great weather. The times I've visited Canada have been wonderful experiences, but I would never comment on any aspect of the country's infrastructure, since I really know nothing about your daily living environment. This article has nothing to do with Donald Trump being President, and everything to do with seeing how the infrastructure of California has deteriorated given the politics of California. I have been a resident of California for 50 years, so I have seen much change and the deterioration of what was once a great state of this nation.

Lorna Harris
11/4/2018 12:48:05 pm

Ms Torres:
Your statements are correct, and some people have stated they would vote a GOP governor if they were like Arnold. I voted for Cox. I am not a fan of Gavin and Kevin De Lone because of their egos and not having common sense. Our so called leaders in CA work for themselves, and their donors. We are being taxed to death and our infrastructure is none thanks to Brown and the DEMs. If the gas tax stays it will go up another 7%. We are taxed every time we renew our car insurance. and my insurance company informed me last July. Where is our money going?

Tony DCCO
11/5/2018 07:44:59 am

Obviously you are not paying for all the free stuff being given away. I believe you stay too long in California, USA, getting some of the "free stuff". Stay in Canada!

Joe Loreylink
1/17/2019 06:47:50 pm

Is that the best you got Gordy? Considering where you are from, it's obvious you don't know squat about the real CA. Perhaps you might learn a little respect for people that obviously know a heck of a lot more than you. And you better be careful here in America about your attitude toward our Commander in Chief. There might be some of us that would take offense to your negative comments...eh?

Monroe Wingate
9/25/2018 06:15:55 am
This will make you feel very sad, but it's a must read.

Lydia Gugich
10/21/2018 07:29:47 am

Excellent synopsis of the 'state' of California . . . . and Texas. Would love to move except that friends and family are here. But equally as important, often the way CA goes, the nation follows. Republicans need to reemerge and fight for our beautiful state. And remember, Gavin Newsom is using the Governorship of CA as a stepping stone to the Presidency!

What good does it do to leave California when Pelosi, Feinstein, and Harris are ruling the country?

Lorna Harrislink
11/4/2018 12:31:03 pm

Ms. Gugich:
How is Pelosi, Feinstein, and Harris ruling the country? Trump, is ruling the country and is doing an excellent job.

John
10/28/2018 02:12:49 pm

Great article! I moved away for my career many years ago, but had the opportunity to take over the family home is So. Cal. in 2013. I was tempted as I had grown up on the beach there. But, I took a drive from the harbor area to S.F. Valley to visit my grandparents' graves on a Saturday, on surface streets. That made up my mind! Nothing but dilapidate stucco buildings, trash, graffiti, bars on windows, potholed rough streets, not a sign in English across much of the L.A. Basin, and even into the S.F. Valley! Will never go back!

Jennifer Pignone
11/4/2018 02:51:27 pm

I would love to share this . This letter is the absolute truth. Everyone needs to read this .

Debra M. Prisk
11/4/2018 05:19:41 pm

You missed how the Dems cheat at the voting polls. Thus making it impossible for us to get a Republican voted in.
https://www.facebook.com/markpmeuser/videos/1166080166873671/?__tn__=%2Cd%2CP-R&eid=ARDjL7UK3D_qWKhC2evdKWVdFMaPdsPhCtXIjtnZoBfOAET-zyH_Cwx_bQcC0FQ27oxtTmwyy8b9Gr4g

and

https://www.facebook.com/markpmeuser/videos/1229858820505589/
just go on Mark Meuser's FB and watch his videos...

Stella
11/8/2018 06:33:33 pm

But a Marine that is not an illegal alien just murdered 11 people in the
state of California. Someone who fought to protect this country just killed
11 people. That's fine. Totally okay. People need to look at the bigger
picture. Love your neighbors. We're all on the same team.

PADDY MCMORROW
11/25/2018 04:25:59 pm
He did not kill them because he is a Marine; he killed them because he is
a sick man! You don't ban cars when a driver kills someone while drunk!

Tony Verreoslink
12/21/2018 08:04:51 pm

Well - actually - the same people who want to ban guns, would probably
love to ban cars as long they can keep theirs, or take Uber, or some public
transit money pit alternative. Sometimes their socialist communist
philosophy just comes face to face with reality, but nothing else will ever
make them back off.

Robbielink
11/12/2018 05:18:13 pm

I left California last year and moved to Florida. I lived in California since
1969. I sold my house in San Diego and paid cash for my new house
here. I had money left over.

M A Serkin
11/19/2018 02:35:17 am

I have read and reread this article, and... I have been forwarding it to
every clear-thinking Conservative that I know, who lives in California. I

can see how Conservatives in the once-great State may feel disenfranchised, but it is not too late to MOVE TO FLORIDA, where we (count every vote) still outnumber non-Conservatives at the Polls - but by the slimmest of margins. With our State Election finally behind us, and Governor-elect DeSantis and Senator-elect Scott, having survived the 'recount storm', NOW is the time to reach out to fellow Conservatives and let them know... FLORIDA is alive and Open For Business. We need THEIR Vote.

Bob Hughes
11/20/2018 08:07:36 am

Unfortunately this is a cancer that will spread to the rest of the country as this is the game plan for the National Democratic party. It is not enough to say let California go down as we will also go down with it, eventually. Conservatives must step up to stop this slide down the slippery slope.

Manny
11/24/2018 01:38:22 pm

Its a shame especially southern California, When I got out of the service I wanted to settle there but because all my family lived in northeast I decided to go home but always hoped to go back.

Tony Verreoslink
12/21/2018 09:37:02 pm

We still have lots to learn.

Ross
1/12/2019 01:02:54 pm

Finally, a concise article that is irrefutable regardless how the libtards spin it!

We want to move out now blacken landscape that was once called a state! However, senior citizen status and medical needs outweigh looking around in another state. We unfortunately need to have a very private solid medical comfort zone.

Unfortunately, we are totally disgusted with the absence of leadership and the absolute failures of the Democratic machinated disaster they have created these last 4-decades.

Nevertheless, the majority of our practitioners avoid state and federal controlled programs because of the profit concept and abusive control mechanisms that create delays and magnifies medial conditions into the more comprehensive situation!

Furthermore, freebie, feel-good ill-managed socialistic crap programs have never once solved a social issue anywhere in our world.

References - Cuba and Venezuela are perfect examples of failure.

--- End of comments section ---

Chapter 14 Remember How We Got Here.

Please take note that the title of this book is Hasta La Vista California.

Construction begins on San Diego border wall with 'anti-climbing plate

Conclusions and Final Thoughts

Here we are at the end of nice sized book that clearly paints California as a state or perhaps some would like to call it a an independent country trapped inside of a huge government to which it does not want to belong. This "country" has been longing for its independence for some time and it shows itself by the laws enacted in Sacramento which clearly would not fly in Fly-Over Country.

At the same time, this book provides another theme that at one point in time—not too, too long ago, there was no nicer state in the Union than Caliminifornia. This word is my cutesie way of referring to the Golden State at the time I moved into my twenties—a bit less than fifty years ago. As you may recall, I wrote in the early chapters about how much I loved the California of fifty years ago. I am sure many others felt / feel the same as I at first look. What a beautiful state it was for sure.

I outlined how my perception changed as the state changed from first visit to last. Now, I find that there are about zero things that California does that I like and so my warm feeling for the state like the warm feelings of many of my friends from "fly-over-country" has disappeared.

I see a California, that is out of touch at almost an insane level with the bulk of the American people. Because of their reticence to enforce the laws of the nation, the state is already overrun by illegals. Its policies show it is against keeping illegal aliens out of the rest of mainland USA. I am for America and Americans first and so on this issue, California and I do not see eye to eye.

When several weeks ago, I heard a caller on Rush Limbaugh suggest that the US tear down the border fence between California and Mexico and give California what it wants—a state with free and open borders with Mexico, after consideration I agreed. It was tough to swallow at first as it would overall be a bad idea if it were not for Calexit on the horizon.

Consequently, I am for Cal-Exit and the secession of California from the Union. With all the debt California has accumulated, executing programs that I would object to funding, I want nothing to do with California philosophies and policies. I want California on its own.

It is like how you treat an adult child who is obstinate and won't agree with common sense. You put them out on their own and make them live the life they have chosen over your objections. Of course, the medical community has this problem well-diagnosed. The technical term for what California is suffering regarding the "Other 49" is similar to Oppositional defiant disorder—ODD.

Oppositional defiant disorder (ODD) is a disorder found primarily in children and adolescents. It is characterized by negative, disobedient, or defiant behavior that is worse than the normal "testing" behavior most children display from time to time. Most children go through periods of being difficult, particularly during the period from 18 months to three years, and later during adolescence. These difficult periods are part of the normal developmental process of gaining a stronger sense of individuality and separating from parents. <u>ODD, however, is defiant behavior that lasts longer and is more severe than normal individuation behavior, but is</u>

not so extreme that it involves violation of social rules or the rights of others.

Does that sound like what you learned about California in this book? For the rest of us, our solution is to separate ourselves from this disorder and chaos by permitting California to do its own thing.

The mental health professional's handbook, Diagnostic and Statistical Manual of Mental Disorders , fourth edition, text revision (DSM-IV-TR), classifies ODD as a disruptive behavior disorder. You may read more at http://www.minddisorders.com/Ob-Ps/Oppositional-defiant-disorder.html#ixzz5mUd7BBNK

After Calexit is approved by the rest of the states of the nation, I would like to see the "Other 49" build a border wall between California and Nevada / Arizona and that wall should be paid for by California the country or New California as part of Mexico. That would be part of the *escape for US* deal. Any county that is not Democrat such as Northeast California—as perhaps Sierra county, as far as I am concerned could attach itself to the US before the wall is built as long as the county borders either Arizona or Nevada. Otherwise, sorry Charlie.

From my perspective, continuing to give the current third world state of California the respect that a US state should have with regard to all other US states, is folly. California wants to dump the US and the US would be far better off letting it happen. It would be another 100 years before Democrats in the new right-sized US would be able to win a national election. That suits me fine. How about you?

A final note of farewell to California from the USA

So long, farewell, auf wiedersehen, goodnight
I hate to go and leave this pretty sight

So long, farewell, Auf Wiedersehen, adieu
Adieu, adieu to you and you and you

That's about as final and as cute as I can make it.

Dear California, please do not think we, the "Other 49" in the US are kidding.

Good riddance.

As the one-time Governator would say:

Hasta La Vista Baby!

Hasta La Vista California –
the sooner the better!

Other Books by Brian W. Kelly: (amazon.com, and Kindle)

Hope for Wilkes-Barre-John Q. Doe Next Mayor of Wilkes-Barre PA: The John Doe Plan, will help create a better city!
Democrat Secret for Power & Winning Elections: Open borders & amnesty add millions of new Democrat Voters
The Cowardly Congress Whatever happened to Congress doing the work of the people?
Help for Mayor George and Next Mayor of Wilkes-Barre How to vote for the next Mayor Council abbreviated
Ghost of Wilkes-Barre Future: Spirit's advice for residents about how to pick the next Mayor and Council
Great Players in Air Force Football: Air Force's best players of all time
Great Coaches in Air Force Football: From Coach 1 to Coach Troy Calhoun
Great Moments in Sir Force Football: From day 1 to today!
Great Players in Navy Football: Navy's best including Bellino & Staubach
Great Coaches in Navy Football: From Coach 1 to Coach #39 Ken Niumatalolo
Great Moments in Navy Football: From day 1 to coach Ken Niumatalolo !
No Tree! No Toys! No Toot Toot! Heartwarming story. Christmas gone while 19 month old napped
Government Must Stop Ripping Off Seniors' Social Security!: Hey buddy, seniors can no longer spare a dime?
Special Report: Solving America's Student Debt Crisis!: The only real solution to the $1.52 Trillion debt
How to End DACA, Sanctuary Cities, & Resident Illegal Aliens . best solution to wipe shadows in America.
The Winning Political Platform for America Unique winning approach to solve the big problems in America.
Lou Barletta v Bob Casey for US Senate Barletta's unique approach to solving the big problems in America.
John Chrin v Matt Cartwright for Congress Chrin has a unique approach to solving big problems in America.
The Cure for Hate !!! Can the cure be any worse than this disease that is crippling America?
Andrew Cuomo's Time to Go? "He Was Never that Great!": Cuomo says America never that great
White People Are Bad! Bad! Bad! Whoever thought a popular slogan in 2018 would be It's OK to be White!
The Fake News Media Is Also Corrupt !!!: Fake press / media today is not worthy to be 4th Estate.
God Gave US Donald Trump? Trump was sent from God as the people's answer
Millennials Say America Was "Never That Great": Too many pleased days of political chumps not over!
White People Are Bad! Bad! Bad! In 2018, too many people find race as a non-equalizer.
It's Time for The John Doe Party… Don't you think? By By Elephants.
Great Players in Florida Gators Football… Tim Tebow and a ton of other great players
Great Coaches in Florida Gators Football… The best coaches in Gator history.
The Constitution by Hamilton, Jefferson, Madison, et al. The Real Constitution
The Constitution Companion. Will help you learn and understand the Constitution
Great Coaches in Clemson Football The best Clemson Coaches right to Dabo Swinney
Great Players in Clemson Football The best Clemson players in history
Winning Back America. America's been stolen and can be won back completely
The Founding of America… Great book to pick up a lot of great facts
Defeating America's Career Politicians. The scoundrels need to go.
Midnight Mass by Jack Lammers… You remember what it was like Great story
The Bike by Jack Lammers… Great heartwarming Story by Jack
Wipe Out All Student Loan Debt--Now! Watch the economy go boom!
No Free Lunch Pay Back Welfare! Why not pay it back?
Deport All Millennials Now!!! Why they deserve to be deported and/or saved
DELETE the EPA, Please! The worst decisions to hurt America
Taxation Without Representation 4th Edition Should we throw the TEA overboard again?
Four Great Political Essays by Thomas Dawson
Top Ten Political Books for 2018… Cliffnotes Version of 10 Political Books
Top Six Patriotic Books for 2018… Cliffnotes version of 6 Patriotic Boosk
Why Trump Got Elected!.. It's great to hear about a great milestone in America!
The Day the Free Press Died. Corrupt Press Lives on!
Solved (Immigration) The best solutions for 2018
Solved II (Obamacare, Social Security, Student Debt) Check it out; They're solved.
Great Moments in Pittsburgh Steelers Football... Six Super Bowls and more.
Great Players in Pittsburgh Steelers Football ,,,Chuck Noll, Bill Cowher, Mike Tomin, etc.
Great Coaches in New England Patriots Football,,, Bill Belichick the one and only plus others
Great Players in New England Patriots Football… Tom Brady, Drew Bledsoe et al.
Great Coaches in Philadelphia Eagles Football..Andy Reid, Doug Pederson & Lots more
Great Players in Philadelphia Eagles Football Great players such as Sonny Jurgenson
Great Coaches in Syracuse Football All the greats including Ben Schwartzwalder
Great Players in Syracuse Football. Highlights best players such as Jim Brown & Donovan McNabb
Millennials are People Too !!! Give US millennials help to live American Dream
Brian Kelly for the United States Senate from PA: Fresh Face for US Senate
The Candidate's Bible. Don't pray for your campaign without this bible
Rush Limbaugh's Platform for Americans… Rush will love it
Sean Hannity's Platform for Americans… Sean will love it

Donald Trump's New Platform for Americans. Make Trump unbeatable in 2020
Tariffs Are Good for America! One of the best tools a president can have
Great Coaches in Pittsburgh Steelers Football Sixteen of the best coaches ever to coach in pro football.
Great Moments in New England Patriots Football Great football moments from Boston to New England
Great Moments in Philadelphia Eagles Football. The best from the Eagles from the beginning of football.
Great Moments in Syracuse Football The great moments, coaches & players in Syracuse Football
Boost Social Security Now! Hey Buddy Can You Spare a Dime?
The Birth of American Football. From the first college game in 1869 to the last Super Bowl
Obamacare: A One-Line Repeal Congress must get this done.
A Wilkes-Barre Christmas Story A wonderful town makes Christmas all the better
A Boy, A Bike, A Train, and a Christmas Miracle A Christmas story that will melt your heart
Pay-to-Go   America-First Immigration Fix
Legalizing Illegal Aliens Via Resident Visas Americans-first plan saves $Trillions. Learn how!
60 Million Illegal Aliens in America!!! A simple, America-first solution.
The Bill of Rights By Founder James Madison Refresh *your knowledge of the specific rights for all*
Great Players in Army Football Great Army Football played by great players..
Great Coaches in Army Football Army's coaches are all great.
Great Moments in Army Football Army Football at its best.
Great Moments in Florida Gators Football Gators Football from the start. This is the book.
Great Moments in Clemson Football CU Football at its best. This is the book.
Great Moments in Florida Gators Football Gators Football from the start. This is the book.
The Constitution Companion. A Guide to Reading and Comprehending the Constitution
The Constitution by Hamilton, Jefferson, & Madison – Big type and in English
PATERNO: The Dark Days After Win # 409. Sky began to fall within days of win # 409.
JoePa 409 Victories: Say No More! Winningest Division I-A football coach ever
American College Football: The Beginning From before day one football was played.
Great Coaches in Alabama Football Challenging the coaches of every other program!
Great Coaches in Penn State Football the Best Coaches in PSU's football program
Great Players in Penn State Football The best players in PSU's football program
Great Players in Notre Dame Football The best players in ND's football program
Great Coaches in Notre Dame Football The best coaches in any football program
Great Players in Alabama Football from Quarterbacks to offensive Linemen Greats!
Great Moments in Alabama Football AU Football from the start. This is the book.
Great Moments in Penn State Football PSU Football, start--games, coaches, players,
Great Moments in Notre Dame Football ND Football, start, games, coaches, players
Cross Country with the Parents A great trip from East Coast to West with the kids
Seniors, Social Security & the Minimum Wage. Things seniors need to know.
How to Write Your First Book and Publish It with CreateSpace. You too can be an author.
The US Immigration Fix--It's all in here. Finally, an answer.
I had a Dream IBM Could be #1 Again The title is self-explanatory
WineDiets.Com Presents The Wine Diet Learn how to lose weight while having fun.
Wilkes-Barre, PA; Return to Glory Wilkes-Barre City's return to glory
Geoffrey Parsons' Epoch... The Land of Fair Play Better than the original.
The Bill of Rights 4 Dummmies! This is the best book to learn about your rights.
Sol Bloom's Epoch ...Story of the Constitution The best book to learn the Constitution
America 4 Dummmies! All Americans should read to learn about this great country.
The Electoral College 4 Dummmies! How does it really work?
The All-Everything Machine Story about IBM's finest computer server.
ThankYou IBM! This book explains how IBM was beaten in the computer marketplace by neophytes

www.ingramcontent.com/pod-product-compliance
Lightning Source LLC
Chambersburg PA
CBHW060901280326
41934CB00007B/1144